"I was determined to shoot all of casting directors and I had 100 speaking parts to cast in only a few short weeks, all of them key. Nearly impossible. Our only hope was to add a local casting director with great taste (who'd bring us only the best actors) with a fast, professional shop. We found everything and more in Lori Wyman Casting. Most importantly, I'm supremely proud of every performance in RECOUNT. We owe much of that to Lori.

So grateful to you, Lori!"

Jay Roach - Director - "RECOUNT" HBO Movie

"Lori Wyman is not only a phenomenal casting director with great taste and awesome resources, she has this truly inspiring and magical quality about her that makes her clients feel comfortable, calm, and centered. Lori's attention to detail, sense of humor, open— mindedness, and tremendous dedication to the directors she works with makes the casting process a truly rewarding journey."

Brian Hecker - Director - "Bart Got A Room"

"A superb casting director like Lori Wyman must have a director's eye for talent, a producer's stamina, and, most of all, a love for actors. Lori also has another rare gift: the instinct to fill even the smallest role with the perfect actor. What she knows about acting and showbiz could fill a book — and now it has. For anyone interested in the craft of performance, in how to audition and get the part, and in how to prepare for a role, Lori Wyman's wisdom will prove invaluable."

David Frankel - Director - "Marley and Me"

The Organic Actor

Insider's Secrets
To Auditioning For Film and Television

Always pursue your passion so you can live your dream,

Lori S. Wyman, C.S.A.

authorHOUSE®

AuthorHouse™
1663 Liberty Drive, Suite 200
Bloomington, IN 47403
www.authorhouse.com
Phone: 1-800-839-8640

First published by AuthorHouse   10/2/2008

ISBN: 978-1-4343-6215-5 (sc)

Printed in the United States of America
Bloomington, Indiana

This book is printed on acid-free paper.

Cover photos by Bob Lasky – www.boblasky.com

I dedicate this book to all the actors out there who are pursuing their passion and following their dreams. As Jack Canfield says in the very first *Chicken Soup for the Soul* book: "Don't let anyone steal your dreams. Follow your heart, no matter what."

Acknowledgements

I have a lot of people I want to acknowledge for helping me write this book. Over the years I have had a lot of teachers and creative influences in the movie business. Each and every one of them has gotten me closer to my personal goal of writing this book.

First, I want to thank my students, for it is they who inspired me to get my creative juices flowing to get this book out there.

To my very first bosses in this business at the ACT I Talent Agency, Peggi McKinley and Stella Freed. They believed in me, giving me my first job in this industry right out of college. They taught me about balance and hard work and having fun. I will be forever grateful to them for opening the door to this great career.

To Chris Morgan, the third-season producer of *Miami Vice*, who took me to dinner and made me look at my goals and take action.

To the many producers and production companies, too numerous to name here, that have hired me over the past three decades, thus giving me the opportunity to continue pursuing my passion of casting.

To David Rubin, casting director at large, who gave me my first real movie to cast and who continues to demonstrate belief in me by bestowing upon me wonderful projects.

To the many wonderful assistants I have had over the years who have been there to propel, cover, clean up and support me. Ken Lazer and Melanie Hartford, I know I would not be as far along in my career if you two had not been behind me all the way. Thank you, also, Ethan Smith, who continues today to be there for me where the others have left off.

To my current assistant, Phyllis Karpinski, thank you for being so supportive and loyal and dependable and trustworthy. You are always there for me and I really appreciate it. Your scriptwriting talent did not go wasted on me. You have helped me edit this book and come up with some wonderful wording. You say just the right words in the right places.

Thank you to Ann McIndoo, my writing coach. She was the one who finally got this book out of my head, onto the tape recorder and into manuscript form. She continues to coach me on this book and I look forward to her continued guidance.

Dear Jean. Thank you for coming in at the last minute and fine-tuning my manuscript so everything looks just perfect. I got very lucky when you walked into one of my workshops. I know we will be there for each other for years to come.

To the many friends and students, too numerous to mention, who have read different morsels and given me feedback. Jessica, thank you for sharing your elementary education teaching degree with me, while working out the kinks in several of the morsels.

A very special thank you to Judie Oron. She is an accomplished writer and a true friend. Her words of encouragement, helpful writing tips and love have carried me through this project. She opens my eyes to new possibilities and makes me see things when I cannot. I'm glad we've grown as close as we have over these past few years.

To Bob Lasky, thank you for making me look so good in your fabulous photos. I must gratefully acknowledge Bob for taking the wonderful book cover photo of me and for also helping me edit the morsel on headshots. Your expertise is most appreciated, not to mention your undying friendship. I know I can count on you always and just knowing you are there for me is a true blessing. I got lucky when I met you so many years ago.

I cannot forget my family. My mother, whom I will always treasure and love and know she is up there somewhere watching over me. She believed in me and told me I could do anything I wanted. My father, whom I love dearly. I admire and respect him and am grateful to have him as my daddy, for I know there is no more honest and loyal man out there. He has taught me about business and shown me how to hold my head up and keep moving forward. To my sister, Marjorie Morhaim, with whom I have had the utmost joy in sharing a life and this crazy business. We have learned from each other and we continue to banter back and forth about life's great obstacles.

To my little Ali Beth. I am so grateful to be your mommy. When many of my friends were sending their children off to college, I was changing your diapers. I never thought I would have any children and then you surprised me. My little miracle. You continue to show me what life is really all about and to stop and take time to smell the roses, or in your case, to catch the lizards. I love you more than life itself.

I have saved the best for last. To my extraordinary husband, Marc Macaulay. You are truly a gem. You are also one of the best actors I have ever come across. It is your stories that have inspired hope in the actors I teach. Your auditioning genius is matched by none. I thank you for introducing me to macrobiotics so many years before we were even a pair, which ultimately saved my life. It is you who turned me onto this whole *organic lifestyle*. You are my biggest fan, my number one support team. Your belief in me, that I can get this book out there, has kept me going. I look forward to building our log home on our mountain property and to spending the rest of our years enjoying what is really important: life together. I love you.

Preface

I have been teaching for over twenty years and casting for almost thirty. I have had the utmost pleasure inspiring and educating actors through my teachings. Every time I finish one of my intensive weekend workshops, someone tells me that this information is so valuable, I should write a book. The students were the original impetus to get started on this book project.

I want to explain a little bit about this book before you begin. Why *The ORGANIC Actor*? According to *Encarta World English Dictionary*, the definition of Organic is:

1. relating to, derived from, or characteristic of living things
2. occurring or developing gradually and naturally, without being forced or contrived
3. intrinsic: forming a basic and inherent part of something and largely responsible for its identity or makeup
4. naturally efficiently organized: consisting of elements that exist together in a seemingly natural relationship that makes for organized efficiency. Need to integrate the various functions of the department into an organic whole.

Isn't that what acting should be? It's the sum parts of the whole. The ORGANIC whole, in this case. You have to act naturally. It has to flow and not be contrived. The acting cannot be forced or pushed. Your performance has to be seamless. We cannot "catch you acting" at any moment of your performance, otherwise it loses the whole effect. Even in your meetings with clients, the conversation has to flow.

Another thing you may notice in this book is that I repeat myself. Why do I repeat certain things? Because I feel they are important and I don't want you to miss them. If I emphasize something in several morsels, I am hopeful it will sink in and you will get it.

In my opinion, you cannot hear good advice too many times. I'd rather you hear it many times and it penetrates, than you miss it and make a mistake that costs you a job.

Why do I call the chapters *morsels*? I do this because they are little bits of information. Each morsel can be digested in a few moments, as opposed to a full chapter, which may need a lot more time to read and process. I realize you have busy schedules, but if you are on your way to a casting and you just need that one little tidbit of help, you can consume it in the car on your way.

I have made this book as easy as I can so that you can grasp each concept and apply it. Keep this book with you. Read a morsel or two each day. Apply the principles of each one. You will see that your career expands just by taking the suggestions in this book.

Table of Contents

Morsel #1: Introduction..*1*
    Who is Lori Wyman?
    Difference between talent agent and casting director
    How this book will enhance your acting career

Morsel #2: It's Just My Opinion *7*
    How did she know?
    One opinion can cause an awful lot of grief
    One person's opinion can change the whole climate of the casting session
    An opinion is not a fact, so don't take it personally
    It is possible to change someone's opinion
    Don't limit yourself, always audition

Morsel #3: To Submit Or Omit.. 15
    Do I submit to everyone?
    I am hired for my expertise
    Responsibility to my client
    If you are not brilliant, there is no reason for me to submit you
    Get your sides in advance
    If you look good, I look good
    Why does a casting director keep bringing you in?

Morsel #4: What's The Plan? 23
    Do you have one?
    What do you need to do?
    Skills of an actor
    Become an extra
    Get an agent
    Submit your headshot, write your résumé, your calling card
    Have a calendar

Morsel #5: How To Get An Agent *29*
    Headshot with a cover letter
    The personal touch works
    Call the agency
    Registration policies
    Most important person
    Don't take "no" for an answer!
    The agent works for you
    Good agent relationships
    Book something directly and then give the commission to the agent

Morsel #6: How To Get Someone To Notice Me *35*
    What works to get attention?
    What is the CSA?
    Best times to stop by a busy office
    The squeaky wheel gets the oil
    Get noticed in a positive way

Morsel #7: Smile Pretty *41*
    What is a headshot?
    The first tool that you will need in this business is a headshot
    How to choose a photographer
    Personality is very important
    Comfortable in your own skin
    Do not drastically change your look
    Professional makeup artist
    Two or three different looks
    Remember, headshot says actor for acting, composite card says model for print work
    Who is a model?
    Trust the opinion of your photographer
    What is a contact sheet?
    Tools for viewing thumbnails
    This picture can mean the difference between getting an audition or not

Morsel #8: Websites *51*
    What should be on your website?
    Music is another important factor
    Someone who builds websites for actors
    Buy your name at Godaddy.com

Morsel #9: Demo Reels *57*
    What is a demo reel?
    What a demo reel is used for
    Examples of good and bad demo reels
    Many generation tape
    How long is the demo reel
    Pick footage for a demo reel
    What is it and how to get upgraded?
    What if you have nothing yet?
    Put your demo reel on your website

Morsel #10: Résumés *65*
    What is a résumé?
    Why do you want a résumé?
    What to put on your résumé?
    How to build a résumé?
    Attaching your résumé to your headshot
    What not to include on your résumé
    The résumé is you on paper

Morsel #11: Scammers *75*
    Who is a scammer?
    Listen to your gut
    Don't sign anything without a lawyer

Morsel #12: Becoming Union: SAG Versus Non-SAG *81*
    How to become union?
    SAG as opposed to AFTRA
    Definition of non-union
    Right-to-work state
    Member in good standing
    "Financial Core"

Morsel #13: The Most Important Person 89
    Who is the most important person?
    Jobs of the secretary/assistant
    Treat everyone with equal respect

Morsel #14: Extras And Such 95
    You have to start somewhere
    What is an extra?
    What you learn as an extra?
    "Back to one"
    What is a stand-in?
    What is a photo-double?
    Different kinds of extra work

Morsel #15: Getting The Call 101
    When the call comes in
    Questions you must ask before a casting
    What you need to know

Morsel #16: Sides 107
    What are sides?
    How do we mark them?
    Make sure you have all of the pages
    Page numbers vs. scene numbers
    How to read sides
    "int" "ext"
    Beginning, middle, end
    Day player
    What is a "search?"
    Learn your sides OUT LOUD

Morsel #17: Memorize Or Not To Memorize 117
    Be memorized before going into an audition
    Think of your audition as a test
    How does one memorize?
    Actors Equity
    You MUST always be memorized

Morsel #18: Dress The Part... 125
    Give the illusion, but don't dress in "costume"
    What colors should you wear?
    Get information on your character

Morsel #19: They're Not Just Props 131
    A prop is a wonderful thing if used correctly
    A simple prop can enhance your audition
    What do you do with your arms and hands?
    "KISS" – Keep it sweet and simple
    Work with your props before your audition
    Look for clues in your sides

Morsel #20: Slating In Character... 139
    What is slating?
    What are profiles?
    What is important about slating?
    You have one chance to make a first impression
    Be as close to your character as possible
    Accents on a slate

Morsel #21: Be In Character, Stay In Character 145
    "Never let them catch you acting"
    The same applies to accents
    Stay in character

Morsel #22: Be On Time 149
    Time is money
    Be early if you can
    What is a read-through?
    Be courteous of time
    Tardy behavior reflects badly on you, the casting director, the talent agent

Morsel #23: Nerves, Get Out!... 155
    Biggest audition inhibitor
    Nerves are healthy
    Strange examples of getting the nerves out
    Relaxation techniques
    What happened to coping skills?
    Remember to breathe

Morsel #24: Don't Make Excuses *161*
    Excuses are self defeating
    Facially/verbally editorialize
    You are a salesperson
    Excuses are just that, excuses
    Keep excuses outside

Morsel #25: Don't Forget To Breathe *167*
    Concentrate on your breathing
    Consequences of not breathing
    SCUBA
    Calmer, more relaxed, more focused
    Breathing techniques

Morsel #26: Be In The Moment *171*
    Stay in the moment
    Don't get ahead of yourself
    Mind, body, and spirit

Morsel #27: Have Fun On Your Audition *175*
    Your job is to audition
    Going to an audition is like playing
    Look at it as a general read
    Be happy with the way you look

Morsel #28: Perfume And Other Smells That Irritate *181*
    Reasons not to wear colognes
    Sense memory
    Smells can alienate clients
    Hygiene is important

Morsel #29: Sabotaging Yourself *187*
    The art of sabotage is alive and well
    How an actor can sabotage himself
    Other people can throw you off
    Showing up late or on time

Morsel #30: The Waiting Room 195

The waiting room is an interesting space
Don't listen to other actors
The energy is very tense
Time in casting room is not indicative of getting the part
Avoid energy vampires

Morsel #31: Horror Stories 201

Horror stories push a client away
Examples of horror stories
Think before you speak

Morsel #32: Words Can Help Or Harm.............................. 205

How they affect our lives and our careers
Your words and thoughts can make a difference
Confidence comes out in words and thoughts
Change the words you use
Part of the game
"Never let them see you sweat"

Morsel #33: Don't Take Things Personally.......................... 211

She thought I hated her
When a casting director looks at their watch
It gets very tedious behind that camera
Be careful when interpreting the behavior of the client

Morsel #34: What To Do On The Set: Set Etiquette 217

What you need to know before you get there
Once you are on the set
What does call time mean?
What is the A.D., P.A.?
The holding area
Honey wagon
Keep a copy of your contract
If you are the principal
Another faux-pas

Morsel #35: Please And Thank You 225
These little words are so important
Brown-nosing, but in a nice way
Nice to be recognized
There is an art to this business

Morsel #36: Letter Writing 231
Letters of complaint
Make sure it is accurate and sign it
Don't let anger or insecurities get in your way

Morsel #37: Don't Get A Big Head 237
There is no such thing as an overnight sensation
You cannot let your ego get out of control
Save while you are earning money
Today does not determine what tomorrow will bring
Keep yourself in check
How to stay happy

Morsel #38: How To Maintain A Healthy Lifestyle While Working In This Crazy Business 243
How to maintain clear thinking, energy, positive attitude, focus
Macrobiotics
Craft service
Sugar is a contributor to ill health
Foods to avoid
Don't numb your experience by taking drugs

Morsel #39: Never Take No 249
Your job is to get us to say "yes"
Desperation is a great motivator
Never be above begging
When you have nothing, you have nothing to lose

Morsel #40: The Summation 255
The thoughts of a casting director
Take my words and learn them, study them, incorporate them
Thank you!
I wish you much success

1
Introduction

My name is Lori Wyman. I like to introduce myself by saying, "I'm a casting director by profession and I'm a human being by birth." What I mean by that is I bleed when you cut me. I cry when you hurt me. I am human. I am human first and foremost, and there's a very specific reason that I introduce myself that way. I do this because I want you to know that the person you are auditioning for is just like you.

I want to give you just a little bit of background on who I am and where I come from, because I think that's important, so that you know the words you are about to read are coming from a reliable source.

I was born in Miami Beach and raised in Miami. I graduated from the University of Miami with a degree in speech and communications. Right out of college I began working as *the secretary* at what was then one of the largest talent agencies in Miami, Act I Talent Agency. The secretary is the most important person in any office, as many of you know, and the rest of you will understand why I say that a little bit later in the book. As the secretary in that office, I learned a tremendous amount. I learned how to make coffee. I had never known how to make coffee. I answered telephones. I opened mail. I filed pictures. I wrote checks. I put people on tape. I submitted talent to clients. I made sure that the right actors were sent on castings. I was the one who was there all of the time and that is why the secretary is the most important person.

As much as I gained from working at Act I, I wanted more of a hand in the casting process. The reason for this was because many times when I thought that an actor was perfect for a particular role, the casting director wouldn't allow me to send that actor. One time, as an agent, I was given a casting and I knew who the perfect actor was. The casting director would not see him, even though I had already scheduled him. I said, "Please, make sure that you see him." She said she would do it as a favor for me, but she thought he wasn't right. Well, of course, he booked the part.

At the time, that casting director wrote for the magazine *Backstage.* She wrote an article in *Backstage,* saying that she had found the perfect person for that role. I'll never forget that because it really stunned me. Obviously, I'm mentioning it, so it did affect me enough that I wanted to take some action because: A. She hadn't wanted me to send this particular actor, and B. Once he booked the part, she took full responsibility and credit for his discovery.

After working at Act One for about five years, I decided I wanted to be a casting director. The difference between a talent agent, which is what I had become, and a casting director is this: A talent agent represents the actors. A casting director represents the producer or the production company. Just as an aside, there is no such thing as a casting agent. Many times I've heard people call me a casting agent. I am not an agent. An agent represents talent. One is a "talent agent," or one is a "casting director." I direct castings. I went from being a talent agent to being a casting director. I wanted more of a hand in working as a casting director, because I wanted to work with the actors. I love the actors. I love working with them on their audition, dialogue and performance.

One of the casting director companies in Miami was working on a very big, Emmy Award-winning television series and they needed some help. After leaving Act I, I began working for them right away. For approximately two years, I worked as the casting director on that particular television series known as *Miami Vice*. After about two years working on *Miami Vice*, through this casting director's office, the producer of *Miami Vice* took me out to dinner one night. He said, "Leave there and I guarantee you the *Vice* account." Quadrupling my weekly salary was a no-brainer and I was still going to be able to do what I loved doing. I became the in-house casting director for *Miami Vice*.

I'm not going to go through my entire résumé here. You can check it out online, but needless to say, *Vice* catapulted me into a brand new category. I was a casting director. I was a casting director on my own, and I had just finished casting a major network television series. From there, I worked on a couple of other television series in Miami and in Jupiter. I worked on *B. L. Stryker* with Burt Reynolds, which was a wonderful experience. Steven J. Cannell brought a couple more television series to Miami—*21 Jump Street* and *Wise Guy*—and I served as the local casting director on those.

After that, I decided to work independently. Until that point, I had been in-house on the various television series. I opened my own office, and, eighteen years later, I'm in the same location. I have had the opportunity to cast many major motion pictures and television series. I absolutely qualify as an expert in helping you achieve your goal of accomplishing anything you want to do as an actor.

This book will take you from beginning to end, start to finish, spelling out the tools you need, how to get an agent, what to do when you get the casting, and then, when you book the job, what to do on the set. It is absolutely accomplishable. I always say, "Somebody wins the Oscar. Somebody wins the Tony. Somebody wins the Emmy, which means it is accomplishable. If somebody did it before, then you can do it now." All you have to do is believe. I am an absolute firm believer that anything you want, you can accomplish.

You will also notice in this book that I have a tendency to repeat certain points many times in many different morsels. I do this to make sure that these important points sink into your brain. They are necessary to maintain your professionalism and to have a much more productive audition experience.

So often I hear about actors taking classes in which the teacher says, "Look to your right. Look to your left. The person next to you is not going to be in this business much longer, because the failure rate in this business . . ." Blah, blah, blah, they go on and on. Absolutely not true! If you take a class or read a book from an instructor or a writer who tells you that, close that book. Leave that class. You need to believe in yourself. You need to believe in what you can accomplish and I am here to facilitate that belief. We are going to continue on in the rest of this book. Ready? I hope you enjoy the journey on which you are about to embark. I wish you all the success in the world, and I thank you for picking up this book.

Notes

Notes

2
It's Just My Opinion

When I first started out as an independent casting director, I had the privilege of working alongside Bonnie Timmerman, a very big casting director at the time. That was while casting *Miami Vice*. Bonnie was casting out of New York and I worked out of Miami. This lady was responsible for starting the careers of many top name actors. I'll never forget the day we stood at an elevator, waiting for the doors to open. I thought, Wow, it's just the two of us. I have her all to myself. I need to ask her, "How do you know?" What I mean was: How could she look at an actor, watch his performance and know that he was THE one? How could she know this actor was going on to greatness? I wanted to know this. I needed to know. I wanted to understand. Her answer: "It's just my opinion."

That's right, ladies and gentlemen, it's just our opinion! And, it's just the opinion of all of the casting directors, producers, writers, directors. It is just our opinions.

For example, an actor friend of mine went in to audition for a recurring role on a hit television series. He was auditioning with a casting director, director, producer and executive producer with whom he had worked before. He had a great audition and they all wanted him. He booked it. He was thrilled. He shot episodes #1 and #2 and he was scheduled to shoot episode #3 when his agent called. The actor was at home, 9:30 at night, bags packed, getting ready to go to bed in anticipation of a very early morning flight. The agent told the actor he had been written out of the rest of the series. The actor was shocked. He was mortified. He wanted to throw up. He didn't know what happened. He told me that night was one of the worst nights of his life. How could this be?

Over the next several days, he received phone calls from the producers and the director, all telling him pretty much the same things. They all loved him. He was a great actor. He was well liked. He was professional, and they believed he was quite an asset to their production. The writing staff, however, felt differently. After they had watched episode #1, they determined that the chemistry between some of the other actors and this actor wasn't what they wanted. The writers had written it that way, but once they saw it on the screen, it no longer worked for them. They decided to get rid of several of the actors and re-cast. It was just their opinion.

Their opinion caused an awful lot of grief in the homes of these poor actors who were now out of a job. As you know, when you get fired—because, in essence, that's what happened to this guy—not only is your income affected, your self-esteem is, as well. This might have absolutely nothing to do with you specifically. It might have had absolutely nothing to do with anything that was in your control. It will still affect you. These poor actors were now out of a job. They had been told that they would be working pretty steadily for the next several months and it came to an abrupt halt.

As Franklin Delano Roosevelt said, "There are as many opinions as there are experts." You have to know that even though one of the deciding votes—and in this case, the producers and the director—might want you, the other opinion may not want you. You are not any better or any worse. It is just a difference of opinion.

Even though an actor's instinct is to take this personally, you can't. These writers never saw this guy before, so they weren't getting rid of him specifically. They just didn't like that character anymore. It's kind of like the shoes don't go with anything in the wardrobe anymore, so we give them away and buy a new pair that matches. There's nothing wrong with those shoes. You just have no use for purple shoes anymore. It doesn't match your wardrobe.

I have sat in on so many casting sessions where one person's opinion changed the whole climate. Once, at the end of an all day casting session with clients, we began discussing whom to book. We had to do this that evening as the shoot was going to be in two days. Every actor needed to be set that night because the next day they had to send the actors to wardrobe. They also had to get all of the actors' information in order. The booking portion was going along fine and everyone seemed to be in agreement until we got to one female character. All but one person in the room liked a particular actress. However, one creative type liked another actress.

These two ladies were completely different. The popular choice was an attractive, refined, well-spoken woman whose perfectly coiffed hair and business-like manner indicated that she was mainstream conservative. There was one creative person, however, who seemed to gravitate towards another actress with wilder hair, a funky style, and not at all like the other lady. This actress was bohemian looking with a darker complexion and lighter eyes. These two women were 180 degrees apart in just about every way.

The room full of clients went back and forth for about an hour. The creative type client fought for his choice like a pit bull. He wouldn't let go. He made his case when everyone else wanted the other lady. He had all kinds of reasons why his opinion was right and theirs wasn't. He hung on and wouldn't move past this one character until he was able to change everybody's mind. He wasn't satisfied that everybody was tired and they just let him have his way. He wanted to change their minds. Even when they said, "OK, fine," he needed them to actually see his point. It wasn't enough that they just went along to move forward. He wanted his opinion to be theirs. It was a very, very late night just because this one creative guy absolutely had to change everyone's mind. He finally accomplished that at about midnight.

You have to know, an opinion is not a fact. You can persuade someone to change theirs. As noted journalist, author and Washington correspondent Elizabeth Drew said, "The world is not run by thought, nor by imagination, but by opinion." That quote is certainly alive and well in our business.

Many years ago I was casting a TV series and we were looking for the character of a criminal attorney whose name was Klein. I asked the producer if he wanted a Jewish Klein or a German Klein, as the name could go either way. He was adamant that the character be Jewish, because he was a defense attorney for a murderer. I had an actor all picked out to read for this part, but he did not portray a Jewish-looking attorney at all. At the very least, he could look of German descent. I brought in several actors for this part, all of whom looked like they could be Jewish, but I also brought in this German-looking actor. In the end, he was the best actor and this producer changed his mind and decided he was right for the part. He was booked and the name of the character was changed to fit the actor.

When you're dealing with someone's opinion, it can always be swayed. Nothing's set in stone. How many times have you thought you wanted one thing and when someone presents another side, you change your mind? It happens more than you know in the casting process. An opinion is not a fact. That's the good news.

One actor I know has booked a number of parts for men older, better looking, or with less character type looks than his. He even booked two huge roles that were supposedly already cast elsewhere. He had gone in to audition for a different part, but then he did such a good job that the director asked him to audition for the bigger role and he booked it. Due to the fact that it is just an opinion, it is important for an actor to just get seen in front of the casting director or the director.

After I see an actor, I remember him. I file his performance in the back of my mind and keep it there for future reference. During a series I was casting, an actor came in to read for a day player, meaning the actor would only work one day. It was a small, but important, role. When the actor walked into my casting office, he said he wouldn't read for this small part, as he was much better than this role. He left and never read for that series again, because nothing more substantial came up for him.

I strongly suggest you read for any part you can. Once you are in the casting office, if you do a good audition, you can always ask to read for something more substantial. You have to first get in the room, though.

An actor I know went to a casting to read for a two-line role. The casting director from Los Angeles had seen his photo and decided he might be good for this small part. He auditioned as though it were the role of a lifetime. Once the casting director saw his performance, her opinion of him changed. She asked him to read for one of the leads in the movie and he booked it. This two-line, one-day role turned into a three-month co-starring role. I have seen this happen over and over, so please don't limit yourself just because a role appears to be too small. You never know what might happen, but you need to know that whatever happens is based on someone's opinion. Our business is not an exact science. One plus one will always equal two, but in this business, you always have the opportunity to change the mind of the person who makes the casting decisions.

I was casting a movie when an actress came in to read for the part of a secretary. The secretary was one of those bimbo kinds of secretaries who had three or four words, something like, "Mr. Jones will see you now." Literally, that's what it was. She came in to audition and she booked it. After she booked it, the director decided that Mr. Jones needed his secretary by his side throughout the entire movie. This part, that started as a one-day, several-word part, with this bimbo sitting at a desk, turned into weeks and weeks of work, because someone's opinion changed. Please don't limit yourself.

Understand that an opinion is just that, an opinion. In our business, everybody has one.

Notes

Notes

3

To Submit or Omit

Here's a question I'm asked all the time: "Do you submit everyone who comes into your office to audition for a project?" Well, here goes! The answer is NO. I do not submit everyone who comes into my office to read. Let me tell you how this works. I am a casting director. I am hired for my expertise in finding the perfect actor for a role. The director and the producer do not have the time to sort through all of the potential actors in a particular market. That is my job. That is the casting director's job.

I am hired for my expertise in finding the perfect actor for a role. Did I already say that? I said it again, because that's why I'm hired. What I do is audition the actors. If I feel that an actor is good enough, he stays on the DVD that I submit to the client. If he is not, the client never sees him. You see, if I put a bad actor on the DVD, the client doesn't look at this actor and say, "He's a bad actor." No, the client says, "Lori's a bad casting director."

Clients won't remember a bad actor's name, but they remember mine, because they hired me for my knowledge. They depend on me to guide them to the best possible actors in my town. This is not a personality contest. You could be my best friend, but if you can't act, or you're not one of the best actors for the role, then I will not submit you. Period! End! Please understand that this is a job. I have a responsibility to my client to present the very best actors I can find to them.

Another part of my obligation, for me, is to make sure the actor gets his sides in advance. SAG has a ruling that states: "The script shall be made available to performers at the casting office no later than twenty-four hours prior to their audition." This doesn't mean that I have to stand at my fax machine all day, faxing sides to you, nor does that mean I have to email it, mail it, or drop it off at your doorstep. I do, however, have to make it available to you. I personally fax or email the sides to your agent in advance, in the hope they will get them to you. I do this because I want you to be brilliant. I want you to look fabulous. My goal is not to omit you. My goal is to submit you.

If you have a casting director who does not get the sides to you or to your agent in advance, then I suggest that you get to your casting early enough to pick them up and then go outside to work on them until your audition time. There are several companies that specialize in getting sides to you in advance. The casting directors send the sides to these companies and then tell your agents where you can download them. I strongly suggest that you make sure you know how to get to these companies so that you give yourself the best advantage. If you live a distance from the casting office—in another state, for instance—then I suggest you get to that location the day before your audition, so you can pick up your sides if they're not available online. If you aren't one hundred percent prepared for your audition, then you've wasted all that time and effort you put into getting to the casting. If your audition isn't brilliant, there's no reason for me to submit you to my client.

An actor friend of mine lived in South Florida. He had an audition in the Atlanta area, and for some reason, the casting director, for whom he was going to audition, refused to fax sides to his agent in advance. The actor wanted to be as prepared as possible, so he decided to drive up a whole day before his audition to pick up his sides, which allowed him to study his dialogue the night before. This meant that he incurred an additional cost for the extra hotel night. He had been told that he would be reading for the part of an attorney in a television show. When he arrived the day before the audition, the casting director gave him sides for a white trash, redneck kind of character.

This role change required a wardrobe change, as this was the opposite attire from what the actor had brought. By getting his dialogue well in advance, he had time to go to the local second-hand clothing store, to buy the appropriate wardrobe, to memorize his dialogue, and to give a perfect performance the following day. If he had driven up with an hour to spare before his audition, he might not have been as proficient with the dialogue, and he certainly wouldn't have been dressed appropriately for that particular character. If he wasn't right for the part, the casting director probably would have omitted him from her casting tape. All of that driving, prep, cost and time would have been wasted.

Often times, when you're in a smaller market, there are no sides available to you from the out-of-state casting directors. The larger markets, Los Angeles and New York, make sides available on various websites that provide this service, but the smaller markets might not. Give yourself the advantage. Get there early. Get your sides in advance. Make sure you have the appropriate wardrobe. Just because you go in to read for the casting director does not mean that she or he is going to submit you to their client, but at least you've given yourself a fighting chance with this kind of preparation.

A young man came into my office to audition for a series regular on an upcoming pilot. He arrived at 11:00 in the morning. He did not know his dialogue very well. I could tell that he could be good if he knew it. We went over the sides and he actually was a decent actor, but he didn't know the words. He kept looking down at the sides and gave very little eye contact to the camera. How could I submit this? There was no way and I told him so. I am rather blunt when it comes to casting. I don't want to waste my time. I don't want to waste your time. That was on a Monday, and I asked him why he didn't know his dialogue. He said he'd just received it. This confused me, because this was Monday, and I had sent the sides out the Friday before. When I questioned him further, he told me he had gotten them on Friday, but that wasn't enough time. After all, his nephew's birthday party had been that previous weekend. What?!!! That's plenty of time to work on your dialogue. Why, in my right mind, would I submit someone who didn't know the dialogue when he had received it three days prior to his audition? The answer is, I wouldn't.

I have actually had actors threaten to sue me if I didn't include them on the tape. It wouldn't serve me or my client to omit an excellent actor from a DVD, nor would it serve either one of us to include someone who didn't have a chance at all of being booked. When a client calls me and I'm casting a feature film, they want to see the top three or four actors. They don't have a lot of time. My job is to see lots and lots of actors and to narrow it down to the best few. I've been casting for almost thirty years. I know what is good and I know what is not good. If you are good, then I want to present you to my client. You see, you are a reflection on me. If you look good, then I look good. I want to look good. It's a very selfish act on my part.

Sometimes, it may not be about the acting. I know this is contradictory to what I've been saying. Sometimes, a project is looking for a type. I know I mentioned that in another morsel, but it's important. A type is a certain look. Usually, these people are not professional actors, but they may be the type of character we're looking for. On a television series I was casting, I was looking for a woman who ran a seedy motel. This particular motel was the kind that you could rent by the month, week, day or hour, if you know what I mean. The director wanted a rough, vampy-appearing woman who looked like she had lived a lot. Maybe she had been a smoker, drinker, drug abuser in the past. Maybe she had run a house of ill repute. I had many women come in to read for the part, but they were actresses. They were playing dress-up. They were *acting* like this character. I knew a woman who had done some extra work for me in the past whose appearance fit this description to a T. I called and asked her to come in and read. Just to let you know how close she was to this part, her *headshot*—and I use this term loosely—was a three-quarter shot of her, with her legs spread apart and her hands on her waist. She was attired in leather and chains. Her hair was long and curly. It was bleached blonde with a black stripe down the middle where the roots perpetually needed to be touched up. She smoked skinny brown cigarettes and she had a very deep voice. She was about six feet tall and weighed around 160 pounds. I actually thought she was a man until one day, for identification purposes, I saw her birth certificate. I brought her in to read for the director. When she walked into the room, her appearance made a statement. She couldn't act, though. She was completely memorized and prepared for her audition. She was a true professional, but her acting skills were limited. She actually had come to my office a couple of hours before the audition to work with me, because she wanted this part so desperately. She was so prepared and the director loved her. He knew she wasn't the actress for the role, but she was *the character.* He cast her and then rearranged the dialogue so that the person she was speaking with had the bulk of the dialogue and she just answered in one word sentences: Yes. No. Maybe. OK.

The director loved her so much he had to have her in his television series, so he made sure that the dialogue was rewritten for her. This happens. Think of some of the movies you've seen where somebody speaks English with a very heavy accent and it's difficult to understand them, but they make quite a visual statement. They have a presence, so they don't omit them. They use them, but they rearrange the dialogue to make that possible.

Does this happen often? No, but it does happen. The director cast her because she *was* the person he had pictured for the part. Let's say that another actress walked in with the same type of look, but she had the acting chops as well. Would this actress have been booked? Absolutely. So, if we had auditioned two actresses of equal value in the looks department, but one was a much better actor, the acting chops would win out.

Another thing you don't want to do is accuse the casting director of not submitting you. This has a tendency to put them on the defensive and then they may not bring you in to read the next time they are casting something. I had a wonderful actor who would come in and read for my projects. He didn't book anything, though. I liked him, otherwise I wouldn't have brought him in to read on a consistent basis. I didn't know why he wasn't booking anything, but I liked him enough that I kept bringing him in. One day he came in to read for me and he looked me straight in the face and accused me of not submitting him. As I said earlier, I'm kind of blunt, so I advised him to look in the mirror, as it had nothing to do with me, and everything to do with his performance and attitude. If I was bringing him in to audition and he wasn't booking, then it wasn't my doing.

Please understand that if a casting director keeps bringing you in, they would not be wasting your time. They would not be wasting their time by bringing you in and not submitting you. Yes, we do omit when someone doesn't meet our standards. Remember, only one person can book the part. If we don't feel that an actor can be one of those contenders, then we don't submit that person to the client. That is what our job is all about.

Notes

4
What's The Plan?

If you have picked up this book, then you have some thoughts of becoming an actor or have some occupation in the entertainment industry. So, what's the plan? Do you have one? Do you know what you really want to be when you grow up? You need to have a plan in order to get where you want to go. It's kind of like going on a trip and not knowing your destination. You know you want a beach. There are a lot of beaches in the world. You have to pick one, get information on it, get a map if you're driving or buy a plane ticket, pack your bags with the appropriate clothing, get time off from work, save up the money and so on. You need to plan for this trip. Can you imagine you live in Washington State and you decide you're going to go to the beach in Florida? Let's say you're going to go to Fort Walton Beach in Florida. "Where is that?" "I don't know. Well, let's just get in the car and drive. Maybe we'll find it." You'll never get there!

What do you need to do? You need to look at this career as a trip. Let's walk through this. Do you want to be a working actor? Do you want to be a star? Do you want to win an Oscar, Tony, Emmy? Do you just want to be able to pay your bills through acting or do you want to have several houses on several continents? We'll start out with first things first.

You want to be an actor, so you need to have the skills of an actor. Where are you going to get those? Take classes. Get involved with a theater group. Start doing some acting in films and on TV shows. Sounds easy, right? No, I know it doesn't sound easy! You think, "Well, gosh, it's easy for her to say. How do I do this?" If you have a plan, it is a lot easier than you might think. There are lots of websites these days that will tell you where the acting classes are in your area. Look them up and call some of them. Find out if you can audit one. Ask people who have taken classes at this establishment and get their opinions. Usually, the better classes are not advertised in the newspapers, so be aware of those.

If you can get involved in a local theater group, you can network with the other actors and find out where they have studied. Every area has film-oriented organizations. Find out about them. Go online. We have such a wonderful opportunity now that was definitely not available to me when I first started out in this business. There was no such thing as a personal computer. There was no such thing as Google. As a matter of fact, there was no such thing as a cell phone, which everybody needs. There was no such thing as a fax machine, answering machine or a pager. None of these things existed. Now you can get information at the drop of a hat, so utilize the technology that's available to you.

One of the easiest things to do is to become an extra in a movie or a TV show filming in your area. Call your local film office and ask them which projects may be shooting in your vicinity. Ask them who the extras casting company is and get their number. Call them and find out what the procedure is to become an extra. We'll talk about that in greater detail in another morsel. Usually, you just need to send over a digital still or a Polaroid with all of your statistics, such as your name, phone number, sizes and sometimes even your automobile information. The pay isn't the greatest for a day's worth of work, but the knowledge you gain from working on a set is priceless. Watch and listen and be prepared. Talk to the other extras and find out how they might have gotten this job. Find out if they have an agent and get names and phone numbers. This is the best way to get your foot in the door.

Once you are at this point, you will then want to get an agent, but in order to get an agent, you need headshots to submit. A headshot is just that. Usually, it's a picture of your head. Sometimes it is a picture of your face, neck, and shoulder area. Sometimes it is actually a three-quarter shot, which means the shot is from your hips or waist up. When you are going to take a headshot, you must make sure you use a photographer who does this for a living. We will go into pictures in more depth in another morsel. Right now, we're just making the plan. You need a headshot as part of your plan. You don't want to depend upon your neighbor's father who happens to be handy with his digital camera. You also don't want to use a professional photographer who shoots weddings and bar mitzvahs only. There is a special technique to shooting headshots. You really need to put the proper time, effort and money into finding the best person in your area to get the very best headshot you can get. If there isn't a great headshot photographer, then find one who might be close enough to you and take a trip.

This headshot of you will be your calling card. This is the picture that will get you in the door, or not. It is the very first representation of you that the agent, producer or director will see. You have to make it the best possible you. You don't want to have it retouched to the point that it doesn't look like you, but it just needs to be a good picture of you. It's important. That needs to be in your plan. Once you've called around to the various photographers, put aside a certain amount of money to make sure that you can cover the expenses of getting the picture taken and having reproductions made.

Once you have your headshots taken and printed, that is when you'll want to start looking for an agent. You will need to put the résumé on the back of your headshot. What if you don't have any credits for the résumé? Then we come back to our plan. That's why I suggested the extra work and the local theater classes to get you started and to have something to write on that résumé. If you're recently out of school and you did a lot of theater in school, put that on your résumé as well. Agents love to see theater credits, as that says you are an actor. All of this needs to be in your plan. Anything and everything that you want to accomplish in this business as an actor, you put that down in your plan. Even though you might have an agent, it doesn't mean you will get sent on every job that you are remotely right for. You will need to remind your agent that you are out there and you will need to do this in an assertive way without being aggressive and obnoxious. If you can gently remind them by providing a bagel and coffee breakfast or a pizza lunch once in a while, then do that. It might be called "brown-nosing," but it works, so use it.

Please remember, there are thousands of people who want to be an actor, so you have to make yourself stand out from all of the others, in a good way. In your plan, write down the agent whom you want to represent you. You may also make a plan for the show or shows on which you want to appear. Do the research.

When I first opened my office, after working as the in-house casting director for some of the television shows that were filmed here, I set my sights on casting two specific projects: One was a big ad campaign and one was a television show. I wanted those two projects to cast, so I wrote them into my plan. I hounded the people who were responsible for hiring the casting director. I sent my résumé, my promo materials, little toys and trinkets with my name on them. I left phone messages, on and off. I didn't stop until I got a call from both of them to hire me.

I am a total believer that whatever you want, you can accomplish. As I said before, someone wins the Oscar. Someone wins the Tony. Someone wins the Emmy. So, you see, it is possible! If someone else has accomplished the goal, then, it is accomplishable. If it is accomplishable, then you, too, can accomplish it. Please, don't forget that.

In your plan, your best bet is to include a calendar. On that calendar, mark down what you plan to accomplish and the date by which you want to meet your goal. Maybe you don't have anything. You're starting brand new. You need a headshot. Or maybe you've been in this business awhile and you need a new headshot. Open up your calendar and write down, "I want a new headshot by . . ." and put the date. Now you have a date. Now you have a goal. I cannot stress enough how important a plan is.

Maybe you want to interview two or three photographers, so put that on your calendar. Get those people's names. Write their phone numbers down. Call and make an appointment to meet them. Once you've done that, then get your headshot taken. After your headshot is taken, write your résumé. If you don't know how to write a résumé, hire somebody to do it. People will do résumés out there for as little as $25 or $50. You can find people in every aspect of this business to help you move forward. Make sure you write it down and have a plan. Know where you're going. If you don't know where you're going, you're never going to get there.

Notes

5

How to Get an Agent

I debated whether to include this morsel in the book. I thought, Wow, can I be so smug as to tell someone how to get an agent? Then I thought that there are certain things that someone can do to get them closer to getting that agent, so I decided to let you know what those are.

The typical thing people seeking an agent do is send a headshot with a cover letter to all agents in whom they are interested. You put your headshot and résumé, along with a cover letter, into a manila envelope and you mail it out. The agent opens your envelope, along with the hundreds of other envelopes they get monthly, and files it "somewhere over there," until it moves to the next pile. Even if you have a good résumé and are a very talented actor, you could get lost in the shuffle, especially if you're trying to get in with a popular and busy talent agency.

When a wonderful SAG actor, whom I had cast many times, moved from New York to South Florida, there was one talent agency he wanted to represent him. His degree was in theatre and he had done an apprenticeship in a well-respected acting program. He sent his résumé and headshot to that agency five times, but they never responded. One day he approached me to ask if I knew them and if I would make a phone call for him. Since he was so talented, I didn't mind making that call.

The agent informed me that she didn't know him but would see him if I thought she should. He had sent his headshot and résumé out to her five times, and she had no idea who he was! Did the envelopes even get opened? Were they sitting in a pile off to the side, waiting to get opened? Did a young intern open them and toss them aside, never even showing them to the agent? Maybe *yes* to most or all of these questions.

How do you get an agent? How do you make sure that the package doesn't end up in the garbage can or in the *circular file*, as it has come to be known? I believe the personal touch works. Will it work every time? Probably not, but it's better than mailing some random headshot and résumé to a veritable stranger and expecting them to contact you with open arms. My suggestion is to call the agency and speak to whoever answers the phone. That person is very likely to be the same person who opens the mail.

When I first started in this business, I worked at a talent agency. I was the secretary. I answered the phones. I was also the person who opened the mail. I was also the same person who filed the pictures, made the coffee in the morning, watered the plants, made the suggestions to the agents about whom we should send out on castings, whom we should give the direct bookings to and so on. As you can see, I was the "everything." I was the one who was there full time, while the agents would come in late, go out for long lunches and leave early in the afternoons. I was the constant. You want to make sure it is the constant who knows you as well as the agent. When you call the agency, I suggest that you ask that special person answering the phone what the agency's registration policies are.

You will probably be instructed to mail in your headshot and résumé, then to wait for the agency to contact you. Unless you have some remarkable résumé and are well known, you may wait a long time to be contacted. At this point, I say you need a gimmick. This sounds terrible, doesn't it? But it works. So, if it works, then we've got to do it, right? Read on, I'm not suggesting anything illegal.

In the morsel on the most important person, the secretary, I say you need to get to know this person, and you do. This is the person who can put your photo in front of the agent. This is the one who can get you in with the agency. So, for starters, if you don't already know, ask the secretary for a specific agent's name. Find out if there is something in particular he or she likes to eat or where she shops. Find a way to get yourself noticed.

I heard a story many years ago about an assistant director who wanted to work with a particular director. He knew this director liked to eat a certain food from a particular part of the world. This food item was quite expensive, as well. The assistant director ordered a large case of this food and had it delivered to the director with a note telling him that he would do anything to work with him. This assistant director ended up working with that director for many years after that.

How much do you want to be represented by this agent? Think of a time in your life when you wanted something. Maybe it was a boyfriend or a girlfriend. Maybe it was a certain item of clothing or maybe it was trip you wanted to take. Think of the lengths you went to in achieving this goal. You stopped at nothing, right? That's what you have to do to obtain an agent and then, ultimately, to achieve the level of success you want in this business. I always say, as you will read in another morsel, "Don't take no for an answer!" You have to apply that when you are going after an agent, as well.

Let's say you meet with more than one agent and they all want you. This is a wonderful position. Then it's your decision which agent you want to represent you. Trust your gut. It always knows. You want to have a good rapport with your agent. You want to be able to call them when you need to or stop by their office when you want to. If you have any questions, you cannot be afraid to ask them. If you don't consider these people your friends as well as your agents, then you don't want this agency to handle your career.

I had a good friend who owned a talent agency in New York City. It was a larger, well-respected agency. She told me her actors were like her family. During Thanksgiving, she invited all of the actors with nowhere to go to have turkey dinner at her home. She did this every holiday meal. As she explained to me, she had to protect her income. You see, if these actors worked, she made money. One of her actors played the lead on a hit television series. His commission to her paid a lot of her bills. If he left her, which he eventually did, she would lose a large part of her economy. Inviting her actors to dinner was protecting her investment.

That's the kind of agent you want. You want the agent to coddle you, to take your calls every time you call them, to pay attention to you, to make sure you are sent on every casting for which you are remotely appropriate. Please, remember, the agent works for you, not the other way around. If all of the actors represented by a certain agent suddenly pulled out of that agency, that agent wouldn't make any money. It is really important for the agent to take care of you.

You also want to make sure that you keep a good relationship with the agent. I met an actor here in Florida who told me he was signed with one of the biggest, most impressive talent agencies in Los Angeles. When I asked him how much work he was doing in L.A., he said he wasn't doing anything. He had been with that agency for a year—one whole year—and they never called him for a casting. When I asked if he had called his agent to find out why, he said he wasn't supposed to bother them.

Not supposed to bother them?! That's not the kind of relationship you want with your agent. When you are signed with an agency, make darn sure you are sent on any and every audition that you can. This is your livelihood, and in order to work, you must be sent out on every casting.

When you send your materials to an agent, make sure you address the letter to a real person. That's why I suggest that you first pick up the phone to find out the name of the person who receives these items. I imagine if you are reading this book, you get regular old snail mail delivered to your home. What do you do if it's addressed to you, using your name? You open it. What do you do if it's addressed to *resident, occupant,* or *neighbor*? Many times, you throw it out. Every once in a while you might open it, but if it's not addressed to you, you probably don't. That's why it is crucial that you call the agency where you want representation to learn the name of the person who needs to see your materials and then direct your correspondence to them. Make sure you include a cover letter and address the letter to this same person. When I receive letters addressed to *Dear Casting Director/Talent Agent*, I ignore them. I presume those letters are not to me personally. *Dear Sir/Madam* usually gets tossed, also, as I am neither a Sir nor a Madam.

Another way to get an agent is to book something directly and then give the commission to that agent. This will show two things. One, that you are a bookable actor, and two, that you are interested enough in them to just hand them money.

If you follow the examples in this morsel, you will definitely get a lot closer to obtaining your agent. Once you have made a connection with that agent, don't let go until you get what you want.

Notes

6
How to Get Noticed

Getting someone to notice you is a little different from how to get an agent. Obviously, you want the agent to notice you, but you also want other people to notice you, as well. I am a casting director, but I started out in this business as an agent. I have seen so many ways that actors have tried to get my attention. I have seen what works and what does not work. I'd like to share some of these with you in this morsel.

I am a member of the CSA, which stands for Casting Society of America. Apparently, there is a label mailing list of all the CSA members. I always know when I have received an envelope from that mailing list since my member name is different from the actual name that I use. I never use my middle name. I always use my middle initial. Most people don't even know my middle name. When I receive a manila envelope from an actor and they have my middle name on the address label, then I know they are using the CSA's mailing list. If someone has to use the CSA's mailing list, then I know they don't know me. The same goes for receiving an envelope that is addressed to *occupant, resident, Ms.,* or if my name is spelled incorrectly, which happens as well. Then I open the envelope and there is a letter to *Sir* or *Madam*. I am neither a *Sir* nor a *Madam*, as I have said. Sometimes there is no note at all and it's just a headshot.

Just the other day I received an envelope from a New York address. Since I am not in the New York area, it would be hard for me to call this person in for a casting. The headshot had the actor's phone numbers on the back, but there was no agent's information on it. Furthermore, there was no letter or note attached to this photo. I wasn't sure what I was supposed to do with this photo. Since the actor lived several states away, listed no agent, and didn't mention if he's planning to relocate to my area, I really had no choice but to throw out his materials. I hate having to throw out people's materials, but if I didn't ask for them and they are not addressed specifically to me, then I have no choice but to discard them. As I said before, when you receive a letter at your home to *occupant, resident,* or *neighbor,* what do you do with these items? You throw them out! They are not addressed to you. They are addressed to whomever happens to open the mail that day. That is how we casting people feel when we get a photo that is not specifically addressed to us.

I had an interesting thing happen that illustrates my point. I was casting a very successful television series a few years ago and everyone wanted to get in on it. I started receiving headshots from this one young man. He happened to be a terrific artist. I know this because he would decorate the manila envelopes in which he sent his headshots. I must have received one every several days for well over a month. These envelopes were decorated so elaborately that it was obvious he spent a lot of time on each one. I smiled at the first one. I looked at the second one. By the third time, I started to recognize them, and by the fifth or sixth week, I decided to call the actor. I figured if he went to that much trouble, time and effort to do these fabulous art projects on an envelope and then mail them to me, the least I could do was to give him a chance. I called him and got his answering machine. I left a detailed message for him to call me and thanked him for the envelopes, saying that I was looking forward to speaking to him. Do you know that he never returned my call and never sent another letter?! Isn't that weird? I have been asked why I thought that happened and I supposed he got scared.

Many people will call my office and leave a message on the voicemail at 2:00 in the morning. They leave these very confident-sounding messages saying they want to meet me and would appreciate a call back. I do not return those calls. Do you want to know why? I presume those people have absolutely no intention of talking to me, because if they did, they would call during business hours. My outgoing message clearly states that my hours of operation are from 10:00 am to 6:00 pm. Maybe I might be at the office a bit earlier or later than those hours, but I am certainly not working at 2:00 in the morning. Guess what? They know that, too. They are afraid to talk to someone, so they leave a message. When no one calls them back, they can blame their failure to become a success on someone else. They can put it on me, for instance, for not returning their call, saying, "Well, I left her a message and she never called me back!"

My experience is that if you really want to get in touch with someone, you call them or stop by their office just after hours. It usually does not benefit you to walk into the office in the middle of their busy day. But arriving after their hectic day is over and they are quietly winding down and getting ready to leave can sometimes work to your advantage. I do not guarantee that you will get them. I do not guarantee you'll even be able to walk in, but it is the best time of day to get attention if it's going to happen. The first thing in the morning is usually the worst time, as we are just getting in, checking messages, returning calls, opening mail and getting the day started. Lunch is sacred. I, personally, do not like someone hovering over me when I am trying to eat, and most people I know don't appreciate that either. If you are truly going to get some health benefit out of eating your lunch, it should be done quietly without talking. You should just relax and eat slowly. The middle of the day is packed with work. The best time I have found to accommodate a walk-in is at the end of the day.

An actor friend decided to meet a casting director in another state. He had no appointment and just got in his car and drove four states away to meet with this person. He walked into the very busy casting office in the middle of the day, when the waiting room was full of people. When he went up to the receptionist, all she could suggest was that he leave his materials, and if they were interested, they would get in touch with him. This actor was a very talented performer with a long résumé. He called me toward the end of his day and told me he had not met this person and was going to drive home. That was a twelve hour drive, mind you. I asked him how far he was from this particular casting directors' office and he told me ten minutes. I asked him why he took that drive in the first place and he said to meet that person. I suggested that, since this was the end of the workday, he should drive those ten minutes back to the office and walk in again to see if he could have a quick meeting. Sure enough, the casting was done and everyone was winding down. He was welcomed in, his demo reel was viewed, he made a very good impression. He even had twenty minutes of chit-chat. Afterwards, the actor called me back again to talk about his meeting. I told him now he was ready to take that twelve hour drive home. This actor subsequently booked many projects through that casting office.

I am not saying that every casting office or talent agency will welcome you when you walk in, but if you don't try, you certainly won't accomplish this. You've heard the saying, "The squeaky wheel gets the oil," or "The early bird catches the worm," right? These sayings were created because they have validity. You need some kind of gimmick or you need to be around in order to be noticed. If you want to get into an agency, walk in one morning with breakfast. I'm not suggesting a full course meal, but maybe a bag of bagels, cream cheese and coffee. Is it lunch time? Bring a pizza, some fruit or sandwiches. Many times, the agents can't get out for lunch and they certainly don't make time for breakfast in their hectic mornings. A meal brought in is greatly appreciated. Make sure you bring enough for everyone in the office.

You want to be noticed in a positive way. Your goal is to get representation and to have the casting directors ask for you when they have a project. You want your agent to think of you every time something comes in for which you are right. You want this to be your livelihood. You don't want to have to fall back on another career. If you are reading this book, then this is what you want. Go for it! Be creative. Don't stop. Keep sending those care packages. Stop in and don't get discouraged. Be that squeaky wheel and it will happen for you. Make sure you get noticed.

Notes

7

Smile Pretty

One of the first tools you need in this business is a headshot. A headshot is just that, a picture of your head. It may also include your shoulders, bust and even as far down as your waist or hips. This shot represents you. It must be the very best representation you can get while still looking like you.

When researching a photographer to take this picture, make sure you find someone who takes headshots for a living. This is very important, which is why you have read this before. You don't want someone who takes a great still life or does a mean wedding or bar mitzvah. Taking headshots requires a special technique, which includes correct lighting, backgrounds, and looks.

How do you find this photographer? Let's say you are new to an area and you still don't have an agent. Nothing prevents you from calling a few good agents in your area and asking them whom they recommend. The person who answers the phone will surely give you that information. You can also go online and Google headshot photographers in your vicinity. By doing these steps, you will get names of some photographers in your neighborhood. If you have an agent or you know other actors in your area, by all means, ask them who took their headshots. Look at the pictures and see whose work you like.

Once you have narrowed down your selection to a couple of photographers, my suggestion is to make an appointment to meet them. Why? Personality is very important when having your headshot taken—very important. This picture is the key to your potential work. You want to make sure that this is the very best picture of you. It has to look like you, capture your personality, and attract people to you. If you are sitting in front of a photographer who makes you feel uncomfortable, you won't be able to open up. Your smile won't be natural and your body will be tense. If a photographer won't meet you, find those who will. When you go in to meet them, ask to see other work they have shot. If they have a website, look at that. They should post some of their work on the site and you can determine from that whom you want to shoot your pictures.

Make sure you look at headshots of people who are in your category. If you are a female in her forties and all a particular photographer takes is boys and girls under ten years of age, you don't want that person. He may be great with children, but not with women.

Once you have found the person whose work you like and with whom you feel comfortable, then set up an appointment to take your headshot. I refer to photographers as *he* in this morsel, but please know that there are a lot of good photographers who are women. When I say *he*, I do not mean a male specifically. Please know that.

Before you get your headshots taken, make sure you like how you look. Make sure you are comfortable in your own skin. Is your hair the color you want? Is it the right style? Do you need it trimmed? Make sure you don't get your bangs cut too short the day before your appointment. Do you really want to lose that extra ten pounds before you get your headshot taken? Do that before you make the appointment. How does your skin look? Makeup can usually help any skin flaws, but you want to feel good when you are sitting in front of that camera. When you feel that you look exactly like you want to, then make that appointment. If you get your photos taken and you are not happy with them because you don't like your appearance, don't blame it on the photographer. I have heard of actors demanding a re-shoot because they are not happy with their pictures, when all along they were not happy with how they looked.

Do not drastically change your look after your photography session. Your headshot must be an accurate representation of what you will look like when you send your photo to an agent or when you meet a casting director.

If you are a woman, I strongly suggest that you get a professional makeup artist to do your makeup for this shoot. I have heard many women say they don't want to spend the extra money and that they are good with their own makeup. The problem is that makeup in front of the camera is a lot different than everyday makeup or even the makeup you put on for a night out on the town. I cannot say this strongly enough. Spring for the extra few dollars and get someone who knows what they are doing to apply your makeup. Make sure the makeup artist you hire does makeup for headshot photography. You may want to have someone do your hair, as well. This may not be as important as your makeup, and many times, the same person can do both.

I also highly recommend that you use the makeup artist with whom the photographer is used to working. Ask your photographer which makeup artist he or she prefers, before you hire someone on your own. This is important, as the makeup artist will know the photographer's style and lighting. They will also be comfortable with that photographer. These are all small details, but each one of them can make your pictures so much better.

What are you going to wear for this shoot? First, you have to know your type. You will usually get two or three different looks at a photography session. Make sure they are completely different and that they all represent you. Could you be cast as a business person? How about a young mom? The guy next door? Blue collar worker? Police officer? Sexy? Trashy? Thuggish? You might want one shot where you are in a business suit with a more serious look. The next shot might be taken wearing a polo shirt with a collar and a friendly smile on your face. These two looks can cover a wide range of characters for which you might want to audition. Just be sure that this photograph looks like and represents you accurately.

I first started out in this business as a talent agent. I would get hundreds of headshots across my desk every week. I would open the envelopes, look at the headshots and then read the résumés. I would then determine if my office should invite this person in to interview for possible representation. I opened an envelope with a headshot of an attractive older woman one day. Her hair was silver and about shoulder length. She looked to be in her fifties and she had a lovely smile on her face. There were not a lot of ladies in this age group and category back then, so I called her to come into the office and meet with me. When she walked in, I was so shocked! The woman who walked in to the office looked like the mother of the woman in the picture. Her hair was chopped off really short, as opposed to the longer length, and white, as opposed to the nice silver color in her picture. Her face was completely wrinkled and very craggy looking. In person, she looked to be in her seventies, as opposed to her fifties. I explained to her that she should not send this picture out as a representation of herself. She shot back that this picture was the best she had. She liked it and wanted to use it. I then told her that if this headshot were sent out to a client and he chose her from this picture, then that is the woman he would expect to see walk through his door. Not the one sitting in front of me. I told her that if she didn't get new updated headshots of what she looked like presently, then I couldn't send her out on castings at all.

While working as an agent on another occasion, I sent out a composite card to a client. A composite card is a selection of pictures that represent you. A composite is used by models, not typically by actors. Please note the difference. A composite is a compilation of pictures, including full body shots in various wardrobe changes. A headshot is just that: a picture of your head, a waist-up shot or a three-quarter shot. A comp card is just that: a compilation of pictures that represent the many looks you can achieve. A comp card is used more for print jobs, as opposed to TV and film jobs. If you are a high fashion model, a lifestyle print or even a character print person, then you need a composite.

A lifestyle model might advertise a new condominium community and they might be in their fifties. Maybe they're in their sixties and they're doing an ad for a retirement community. That is more lifestyle. The ad would feature attractive people, but they might be in their thirties or forties, as opposed to these high fashion models who are very young, beautiful and skinny!

A character print person might be a burly man in his thirties or forties who is advertising a trucking company. He, too, is modeling, if you will, but he is certainly not a "model."

If you are an actor and your focus is on acting, then you don't need a comp at all. As I said, a comp card usually says *model*. If you are an actor, you would not want to give a film or television project client a comp card. REMEMBER, HEADSHOT SAYS ACTOR

FOR ACTING. A COMPOSITE SAYS MODEL FOR PRINT WORK.

Can actors do print work? Absolutely! Lots of actors do print work, however, it's important that you make sure you know that you give your headshot for acting jobs and your composite for print jobs.

Now back to sending out that composite card. I once sent out a comp of a beautiful girl with long, flowing blonde hair, who looked great in a bikini. The client booked her directly from her composite to shoot a catalog in the Bahamas. She was scheduled to leave at the end of that week. This model called me up all excited the day before she was scheduled to leave and told me she had just cut her hair like Lady Di. I don't know if you remember Lady Di's hair, but it was rather short. This cute, short haircut was very popular at the time, but the client had booked a girl with long, flowing, blonde hair. This way they could photograph it as she ran along the shoreline of the beach. If the client had cancelled her, it would have been no one's fault but her own.

If you are a man and you have facial hair, you may want to have your headshots taken with the facial hair. Then, during your photo session, have shots taken clean-shaven as well. If you always sport the facial hair, then that is how your pictures should look. You will also have to decide if you want color or black-and-white, borders or borderless, headshot or three-quarter shot, from the waist/hip up, and so on. Those questions should be asked of your photographer.

If you have selected the right photographer, then they will know what is *in* at that moment. When I first started out, headshots were of the head and upper shoulders only and they were black-and-white with a thick border. Today, they are color and usually shot from the waist up or even hips up.

Once you have had your pictures shot and received your contact sheets back, you will need to pick out the pictures that best represent you. A contact sheet is a compact layout of your photo session compiled on a single sheet of photographic paper. Each photo is a thumbnail size. Please note that a contact sheet has approximately twenty-five pictures per sheet. You would probably get two to five contact sheets of your session with the photographer.

Ideally, these thumbnail prints should be viewed through a "loop" or magnifying glass. It's a special tool that photographers use to look at contact sheets. You should ask your photographer to help you select the few that he likes the best and take them to your agent, if you have one, to help you, as well. If you don't have an agent, then you should trust the opinion of your photographer, as he or she is the expert. They know what they are doing and you are paying them for their expertise. You need to trust their judgment.

Once you have picked out the shots that will be your calling cards for the next year or so, you have to get them printed. Again, ask your photographer where they would send their pictures to be developed. You would not want to go to your local drugstore. You'll want to print up at least one hundred of each. I strongly suggest at least 250, as these shots can be used up very quickly.

Go to a printer who specializes in multiple headshot reproduction. If you are trying to get representation, you will need to send out lots of photos until someone responds to them. If you already have an agent, they will want to keep many on file. Agents send out your headshots to their clients, as well, and they do not get them back.

On the back of your picture, you'll have to put a résumé. We will discuss résumés in greater detail in another morsel. Just make sure your résumé is printed directly onto the back of your headshot, stapled on all four corners, or glued onto the back.

Once you have gotten your pictures taken, printed and a résumé affixed to the back, you are ready to send them out. Remember, this picture is your calling card. It represents you. This picture can mean the difference between getting an audition or not. Sometimes, agents submit their talent via email by sending pictures only. The more professional the headshot, the better your chance of getting noticed. The cost of getting your headshots can run into many hundreds of dollars by the time you finish with the shooting, makeup, styling and reproducing. You should save up to afford this expense, as it is one of the most important expenditures for your business. This is the first impression that someone will get of you. You know what they say about a first impression? You only get one chance to make one. Make it a good one. Make it the best!

Notes

Notes

8
Websites

We are in the 21ˢᵗ century now, so get with it. It is time that you had a website, as well as all of the other tools of the trade. A website allows clients from all over the world to access you in the blink of an eye. It allows the producer across the country to see your work at a moment's notice. This is a good thing. Your website should relate to this business. If you are trying to promote yourself as an actor, stuntman, voiceover talent or print model, you can have one website to showcase all of these attributes. If you also want to advertise your charter fishing company as well as your house painting business, you need to have these businesses on another website.

What should be on this website? You want to make sure you can include some footage from various projects you have shot. You also want to make sure you have some professional headshots on here as well. This website should reflect your current résumé, headshots and demo reel footage. You may also want to have an autobiography and some interesting information about yourself which pertains to the film business. Remember, this is a business website so don't use it to shout out your views on animal rights, saving the whales or stopping abortions. This should only serve to promote you in the film, television and print industries. You don't want to possibly alienate a potential client. You want to entice them to hire you.

Music is another important factor on your website. Don't forget, we are in the entertainment industry, so you want to make this website entertaining. You might want music to greet visitors. Make sure this music reflects who you are. If you are a female in your thirties, a young mom type who also does voiceovers for children's toys, do not use heavy metal music. If you are a young guy in your twenties who wants to be a rap artist, mellow jazz isn't the right choice for you. Take lots of time in your selection of music, as this is what your potential client will hear from the very beginning of your website. With the wonderful advent of iTunes, you can literally browse all kinds of music and spend days doing this.

I also suggest that you look at the websites of other people who are in your general category. If you are a man in your forties who plays lots of cops, detectives and bad guys, look at websites of men in your category. I do not say this so that you can copy them. I would not suggest that. I say this so you can get ideas of what those who are your *type* do. If you find a website that you like, ask that person who did their website. Don't be timid when it comes to this. This is your business and you need to make this presentation as professional as possible.

Look for someone who builds websites for actors. This would be a good person to help you create yours. There are many web builders out there, but if you find someone who builds websites specifically for actors, he should be familiar with your needs. He knows that your website should be able to show video footage. He knows that it needs to be accessed quickly. In our crazy business, people don't have a lot of time to wait for the website to load and then finally play. The quicker, the better. The web builder also needs to make sure that your website can be accessed by Mac and PC users. This is very important. There are many competent web builders out there who can assist you in this process. Make sure you use one of them and let them show you what they have to offer. You can and should have your own ideas, but I recommend that you also listen to the advice of the professional who does this for a living.

Will this be pricey? It can be. I know an actor who also builds websites for actors. It is what he does as well as the acting. He has done many of these. He charges anywhere from $500 to $750 for the set up and the website organization. He then charges a nominal monthly fee to maintain the site. Is this too expensive for you? Well, think of it this way. If one client sees your professional website and books you for even a SAG daily on a film or television project, your website has just paid for itself. If you book a second project, it's all profit.

As a casting director, I have a website. I cannot tell you how many times, after looking at my website, clients have called to tell me how impressed they are with my credentials. It's all part of the package. We are in a very technical era now and you, as an actor, need to step up to these times. The website is yet another tool that will only help you gain employment in your chosen field.

As soon as you finish reading this morsel, go buy your name as a domain name. If your name is John Doe, as soon as you finish reading this morsel, as you are reading these words, go online and purchase JohnDoe.com. It may already be taken. You may want to purchase TheJohnDoe.com or JohnDoeActor.com or JohnDoeActs.com. Think of all of the different possible combinations that you could use and BUY IT NOW! At this writing, there is a website called GoDaddy.com. There are many others, but you can buy domain names from GoDaddy.com and they are rather inexpensive. Just buy your name now and you can worry about finding the web designer later. I cannot impress upon you enough that you must have a website. Maybe you can create a MySpace site or post your video on YouTube. Whatever you choose, it is imperative that you have a site where you are represented in order for potential clients all over the world to be able to access you.

Notes

Notes

9
Demo Reels

First of all, what is a demo reel? This is video footage of your film or television work. It should be the best representation of you and your work that can be put together. Your reel is comprised of snippets of produced performances compiled on a short, five to seven minute DVD. Some people are now making them even shorter: 3-4 minutes. As I write this, DVDs are what's *in*. If you happen to pick up this book a few years after its publishing date, then make sure you produce your demo reel on whatever the format of the day happens to be. Since DVDs happen to be what everyone is using now, we will talk about that format. Demo reels can be a compilation of any of your commercial, film or television projects. You don't, however, mix your commercials with your film or TV footage.

A demo reel is used for various reasons. It can be viewed by a director when an actor cannot attend an audition. It can be viewed by an agent to determine if they would like to represent that actor. A casting director may view it to determine if they want to bring the actor in to read for a project they may be casting. I have used demo reels many times to show my client when the actor cannot be in my office.

When you are putting together your demo reel, you want to pick footage from projects that you have already filmed. You want to make sure this footage is a good representation of you. An actor came into my office one day and he was all excited about this new commercial he had just shot. He wanted me to look at it. This is what I saw: It was a picture of the back of a couch. Imagine this in your mind. There were two people sitting on a couch watching television. It was a guy and a girl and he had his arm around her shoulders. Realize, I am looking at the backs of their heads while I'm watching this footage. There was a voiceover talking about the product that was being advertised. We never saw the faces of the two people on the couch. It was thirty seconds of watching the backs of two heads! The actor was so excited about this commercial, because he was one of only two people in it. This is not the kind of commercial you want to put on your demo reel. We never saw this actor's face, nor did we hear his voice. This is a BAD representation.

Another demo reel I received was from an actor—and I use the term loosely— who wrote and filmed all of the scenes himself. In one scene, he had dressed as a clown—makeup, nose, wig, etc. We couldn't even tell whose face we were seeing. He had then been tied to a big tree, from where he recited a monologue. In a subsequent scene, he was in a bathroom. The shower was going, filling the room with steam. The medicine cabinet mirror had clouded over and this guy stood in the shower, reciting another monologue over the sound of beating water. I was appalled by this very strange excuse for a demo reel. Needless to say, this is not what you want to use for your demo reel either.

What do you want to use? You want to use footage that was professionally shot for a commercial, a film project or a television show. That is all you want to use. Theater performances do not belong on your demo reel. Make sure the footage you use features you. If you are an extra in the background, walking by while the principal actor delivers his dialogue, you don't want to use this. Always remember, you only have one chance to make a first impression. If this is going to be your demo reel and this is what you want to use to get yourself noticed, make sure it is the best representation of yourself. You want to make sure you don't mix your commercials on the same reel as your TV and film projects. Did I say that before? I am saying it again. It is important. I always get asked, "But, what if I don't have anything else to put on my reel?" Then wait.

One of my best suggestions is to get yourself involved in student films. Even though there is usually minimal or no pay, you can get bigger roles, more exposure, more screen time, and better quality footage than trying to do something on your own. You can contact the local universities and ask to speak to the film school departments. Many of our wonderful filmmakers of today started out as film students at the local universities.

Volunteer to work on set, if you can't get a paying job there. Find out who does the local extras casting in your area. Becoming an extra is a wonderful way to learn your way around the set, make contacts, get yourself noticed and possibly get upgraded to an actual speaking role. If you don't put yourself in the position of being on the set, then you can't possibly get upgraded. Upgraded means you are promoted, if you will, from an extra role to a featured speaking role.

Your demo reel should not be too long. As I said, anywhere from five to seven minutes is more than sufficient. If you only have three to four minutes of good quality work, then that is fine, too. Don't make it too long and boring. Remember that the people who are watching this are used to watching demo reels. You want to hold their attention, to entertain, and excite them about you and your work, and then to leave them wanting more. These are not your friends and relatives who are watching the ballet recital of their five year old! This is business and we will pick very few people from all of the demo reels that we receive.

After you've compiled the footage that you want to use for your commercial demo or your TV and film demo reel, then you want to take it to a qualified person who has experience making demo reels. This will cost you some money and some time, but this is a business investment and a write off. Don't let your cousin who happens to be handy with his computer put your reel together. Find a person who does this for a living and knows exactly how it should be edited together. There should be credits, music, and special effects. It should be edited so that only scenes or shots of you are on the reel. This takes time and precision and you will need to work very closely with the person who is putting this together. A demo reel is not something that you put together that often, so make sure that when you do, it is the best of your work at that time.

I was casting a film project and there was an actor whom I wanted to audition. This guy is a brilliant actor and I knew the director would love him. The actor wasn't available for the session with the director, so the agent asked if she could send the actor's demo reel instead. I was so happy that he had something for me to show the director. When I received the demo reel, I looked at it before I showed the director. It was horrible! What made it horrible? First of all, it was a many generation tape. What do I mean by this? What I mean is that someone had made a copy of a copy of a copy of a tape. The sound was all muddled. The footage was very grainy. It was all greenish. I couldn't even discern where the actor appeared in each scene, and I knew who I was looking for! There was no way I could have shown this tape to the director. There was actually nothing to show him.

This was too bad as I really thought this actor should have gotten this part.

Here's another example of a demo reel hurting an actor's chances for a film casting I did: The actor had been on the original casting but could not make the callback. The actor offered me his demo reel instead. I showed the director the demo reel. It had been poorly edited. The sound was bad and the quality of the footage was shaky. The footage was from Spanish soap operas. The acting in the Spanish soap operas is way over the top when compared to the acting in the English speaking, American market. Not only that, but this actor was auditioning for a project in English and all of the footage on the demo reel was in Spanish. After watching this demo reel, the director decided he didn't want this actor after all. It absolutely had to do with what he saw on the demo reel.

Make sure you present a demo reel with the same kind of acting for which you are auditioning. In other words, don't show a client a comedic commercial demo reel when auditioning for a dramatic film role. You might be the best actor for that role, but if we can't see exactly what we are looking for, we can't imagine it.

You have nothing, you say? Then you need to wait before you put together your demo reel. In the meanwhile, you should be building your résumé of work and making sure you get copies of everything you shoot. This may take awhile, but it is possible. Make sure you get contact information from the clients after each shoot and stay in touch with these people. You may have to badger them a bit, but don't give up until you get that footage. That footage is what will help propel you to the next level. You need this footage to put your demo reel together. It is possible to record it from the television set, but the quality will not be as good, and therefore, your finished product will not appear as professional.

If you appear in a film or a TV program, stay on top of the producers to get your footage. You may need to send a stamped, self-addressed envelope to get this, so do whatever it takes to get the best quality copy of your footage. Once all of your footage is obtained, determine what you want on the reel and then take it to a qualified person to put it all together for you.

In addition, this demo reel is something that should be on your website. Make sure your website has the capability of supporting video, so that when your demo reel is done, you can also upload it to your website. Remember, this is another marketing tool for your career, so make it the best you can.

Notes

Notes

10
Résumés

What is a résumé? A résumé consists of some or all of the following, but is not limited to these things only: your name, statistics, as in hair color and height, union status, agent's name, web address, phone numbers where you can be reached, a list of your credits, acting training, education, and special abilities. This appears on the back of your headshot.

Why do you want this? It is important to have a résumé on the back of your photo so that the client knows your level of expertise. The client likes to know whom they may be hiring. It gives a director a level of confidence if he is hiring someone who has been on a set before, who may have been in other big projects, and who knows how to handle herself on a set. It should be contained on one sheet of paper only and should be pretty simple. You should not print it on fluorescent purple paper with flowers all over it, for instance.

The résumé can tell a client many things. It can tell a client if he wants to use you or not. Let's say that a director sees two auditions for the same part. Both actors are equally competent. He does not know which actor to hire. Then, he may turn the headshot over and read the résumé. One actor may have many more credits than the other one. Sometimes this may work in your favor, sometimes not. If the director wants a seasoned actor, then he would hire the actor with the bigger résumé. Maybe the director wants someone new and fresh, so he would book the actor who has the smaller résumé. A résumé can tell a director a lot about an actor. Let me put it this way: a résumé *had better* tell the director a lot about an actor. He can see other directors who have hired the actor in the past. Maybe he even knows one of these people and then he can get a reference before he makes his final decision.

Make sure you don't put a credit on your résumé if it isn't true. An agent called me for a referral once. Apparently, an actress wanted to be represented by this agency and she didn't have a lot to put on her résumé. She decided to add my name and said that she had done one of the intensive workshops that I offer. I only take about fifteen people in these classes, so I know the people very well in there. This actress figured I wouldn't know the difference or that the agent wouldn't check anyway, so she added my name and class under "training." When the agent asked me about her, I told her that this girl had not taken my workshop. She immediately tossed the girl's materials in the garbage. She wasn't interested in an actress who would lie on her résumé.

Having just told you not to lie on your résumé, I will tell you another story where an actor did just that and it opened doors for him. He didn't have any credits, so when he was first starting out, he decided to find some theaters that were no longer in existence. He found out the whole roster of plays that these theaters had presented. He found several that had roles for his type and he put those on his résumé. He wasn't found out for many years and by then his résumé had grown considerably, because people had hired him based on his impressive theater credits.

Oftentimes, I hear actors who are just starting out tell me that they have nothing to put on a résumé. Think of all the things you have done in your life thus far. If you have ever done a play, even if it was in school, put that down. You don't have to say that you did the play in high school. You just have to put down the name of the play and the role you portrayed. Any musical aptitude you may have, sports you play, extra work you may have done, acting classes you may have taken should be included on your résumé as well.

You might also have a commercial section on your résumé. This is where you list all the commercials you have shot. If you have not shot any, or even if you have shot some, you can just write down, "commercials - conflicts upon request." This way if they are shooting a *Coke* commercial, all they would need to know is if you have shot any other soft drink commercials. You do want to put your college education and any performing arts schools you may have attended. When you have nothing substantial or professional, you put everything you can on your résumé until you start building legitimate credits.

How do you build a résumé? There are so many avenues you can take to start accruing credits. If you'd like to start with theater, you can look in your local newspaper and find the various community theater auditions. They are usually posted on certain days of the month. Agents and clients love seeing theater on a résumé. You can also contact your local colleges and universities. Find out if they have a film school. If there is a film school, then there is a student film being shot. Most film departments will keep headshots on file and when they begin their casting, they will contact you for an audition. This is a wonderful way to gain experience on a film set, get a credit for your résumé and get some footage to begin a film demo reel. Call your local film office and find out what projects may be shooting in your area. If there is a film or television project being shot, then extras will be needed. Find out who the casting director is and call them to find out who is handling the extras' casting. All you need to submit is a snapshot or digital photo to become an extra. This is another great way to add more credits to your résumé. Once you have done extra work for this casting company, you can find out how to stay in their files for any other projects they might be casting.

You may have heard the adage, "Work begets work." Well, it does. Once you are on a set and you start meeting the other extras, you can start networking. Then you will learn who the players are in your area and what projects are casting. This way you can begin to get your name out there. Extra work is a great way to gain experience on a set as well as add credits to your résumé. As you continue to add more and more credits this way, you can then send out your headshot with a much more substantial résumé to bigger and better agents and continue moving up the ladder.

Make sure, though, that when you add extra work to your résumé, you don't label it *extra work*. If you were an extra in a movie and you played a reporter, but there were twelve reporters, you don't need to tell us all of that. All you need to do is give us the title of the movie and the fact that you played a reporter. If you were a nurse, you put *nurse*. Most of the extra work that you do will not have an actual name, but it will be *a reporter*, or *a nurse*, or *a jogger*. Use those titles on your résumé, as well as the name of the movie and the part you played. Do not write *featured extra*, or *extra*. That is not necessary.

How do you attach your résumé onto your headshot? This doesn't seem to be a very hard question, but I do get asked quite often. You can attach your résumé by having it printed directly onto the back of your picture, by printing it on plain white paper, then stapling all four corners, or by gluing it to the back. Just make sure that it will not become detached from your picture in any way. I suggest you have it attached before you arrive at the casting. I cannot tell you how many times an actor has come into my office with his headshots in one pile and the résumés in another. Then he asks to borrow my stapler or my glue stick. This is not the way to do this. If you have two separate items and you hand them into the casting director this way, they may become detached from one another, thus causing you to get overlooked in the pile. Make sure you have done all of your preparation before you walk into the casting office.

I also suggest that you include your phone number on your résumé. Most agents will tell you not to do this because they are afraid that the client might go behind their back to book the job directly, thereby cutting out their commission. I want to tell you why I suggest that you do put the phone number on the résumé and I want to tell you why I am right. If a client wants to reach you after hours and your agent's office is closed, you will want to be reached directly so that you don't miss a job opportunity. I have gotten last minute castings that came in after hours. I have called the agents and reached voicemails, as opposed to that particular agent. If your agent doesn't check messages until the next business day, it may be too late for you to make your way into my office. If you happen to live a good distance away from my office and the agent doesn't get the message until 10:00 the next morning, but the client needs to see you by noon, then there may be no physical way for you to make it. If you knew the night before that you needed to make a three hour drive the next morning, you could plan accordingly.

During a time when I was casting a television series, my office and I were on our winter holiday vacation. I received a call from the producer on the Friday evening before the Monday when we would be resuming work. He informed me that the director would only have Monday afternoon to see talent, so I had to put together a casting session for him at that time. This gave me from Friday night until Monday afternoon to pull it all together. That might not have been too terrible except that this was New Year's weekend. Saturday was New Year's Eve day and Sunday was New Year's Day. I couldn't do any casting over the weekend and every agent's office was closed. I left messages at everyone's office. No one got back to me, so I had to resort to calling the actors directly in order to organize a full day of casting on Monday. I couldn't wait until Monday to do this.

The actors whose direct phone numbers I had, I was able to contact. If I didn't have their numbers, I could only hope that their agents checked their messages over a holiday weekend. When Monday morning rolled around, I had scheduled many actors to come in and read. Most of the agents were now returning my phone calls, but, by that point, it was too late to schedule the actors to come to my office. I had brought in about three people per category and I had only found enough actors for about nine categories. Since we had to cast about twenty-seven roles, the director booked one of the three contenders for the actual part they were reading and then he plugged the other actors into one of the other categories. I ended up casting all twenty-seven parts that afternoon, so basically almost everyone who read that day, got cast. It was a shame that so many people got left out just because I didn't have a direct phone number to reach them. It was also quite amazing how many agents got angry with me for calling them over a holiday weekend. You, as an actor, just want the call. I know you don't care when it comes in. Make sure you can be reached directly.

There are certain things you do not want on your résumé. Some of these include your age, your Social Security number, your weight and your date of birth. These are not necessary to divulge. If a client needs to know your age, give them your age range, but don't put that on your résumé either. A client can look at your picture or at you in person and determine how old they think you look. Your real age is really not important. It is how you come across on film that matters most. There are times when you'll hear of an actress portraying another actor's mother and they are only five years apart. It's all about how you look, not your actual age. SAG actually says that a client cannot ask your age. This way you won't be discriminated against if you are chronologically too old or too young for what the client wants.

When you book a job, the client will need your Social Security number. It is not necessary, however, and actually not safe to put it on your résumé for everyone to see. Unfortunately, we live in a time when there is so much identity theft that you don't want to give anyone any help in finding out your information. When you book the job, then you can give your Social Security number out to the client.

Sometimes an actor will come into a casting and tell me they need to update their résumé, but haven't had time yet. They tell me that they have just shot two more projects. I ask them why they didn't write it on and I hear, "I didn't know I could write on my résumé." Yes, you can write on your résumé. It is better to hand write in two more film credits than to leave them off and then we have no idea that you have done this work. There is no harm in writing in more credits. This actually can look good. It looks like you have been working and that you have been so busy that you haven't had time to sit down at the computer and type in the new credits. I know an actor who had a larger space for the film section of his résumé so that he could just keep writing in the credits. This approach made clear that he was a very busy actor, which he was.

Just remember, the résumé represents you and your work in this industry. It should only have your work in this industry on it. We do not want to know that you have a degree in math or that you make a mean omelet. If you have a special ability and it can relate to this business in any way, then by all means, use it. If you can ride a horse or a motorcycle or if you can skydive or hang-glide, these might be helpful on an acting job. Look at all of your talents and see if any of them pertain to something you could do on film. Then add them. If they are not something that could be utilized for this business, then don't include them. Certified scuba diving is always very popular if you're shooting in Florida or anywhere near a beach.

A résumé is meant to entice a client or an agent to want to work with you. If you don't have enough credits, then your mission is to work towards building your résumé. When you get a better credit, then you can bump an older credit or one that isn't as impressive. As you continue working, you will keep updating your résumé. The most recent credits will go at the top.

The order of the categories may change depending on the role for which you are auditioning. If you are reading for a play, then your theater credits will be the first group of credits. But, if you are reading for a film, then your film and television credits will go first and the theater credits will come next. The last group of credits will be your training and education and then your special abilities or skills. The top of your résumé has your name, contact information, personal stats, such as your height, hair and eye color, and union status.

The résumé is you on paper. Keep it simple. Keep it neat. Everything spelled correctly, especially the names of people with whom you have worked. You will want to proofread and proofread again and make sure that the type you are using is legible. You don't want anything all curly and fancy. Make it plain. Make it simple. Make it legible. This is what the client will see before they meet you. This is what the client may see instead of you if the résumé doesn't grab their attention. Make sure it is the very best representation of you. Build and keep building your résumé. As you keep building your résumé, you will be a working actor.

Notes

11

Scammers

I have decided to add a little morsel on scammers. My definition of a scammer is someone who is trying to get away with something when their intentions are not honorable. I have seen many of them over the past thirty years. Thankfully, I have not fallen for any of their ploys, but I know many people who have.

Let's start with the agents who are not honorable. They usually put ads in newspapers or have little booths set up in the local malls. Most reputable agents would not even think of putting an ad anywhere except in trade publications, which they do only to promote their agency and its people to potential clients—not to gain more talent for their files.

Usually, the dishonorable agents are a one-stop shopping center. They will train you, take your photos, print up the photos into headshots and composites and then obtain work for you. They usually charge exorbitant fees for these items and their work is shoddy, at best. Please, remember, an agent is not a photographer and a photographer is not an agent. You should not go into an agency where they have a photographer on staff. Many of these scam agencies take these photos to bring in income and never have the contacts to actually get you work.

Many years ago the mother of a small child called me to inquire about children's classes. At the time, our class consisted of about ten hours of training for about $15 per hour. This was the right amount of money for that time. When I told this woman the cost of the class, she just flipped out on me over the phone. She raved and ranted how she was tired of everyone trying to get money out of her. When she told me that her child was only eighteen months old, I told her that we didn't even train children that young anyway. The reason she had become unglued is that she had seen an ad in the paper and called the agency that was advertising. She brought her baby into the agency and paid $800 to get photos taken of her child. The agent/photographer told her that they were going to print up six hundred copies of the composite, but they were going to keep them all so that they could send them out to all of their clients. This way they could try to obtain work for the eighteen-month-old child. I asked this woman if she had any of these pictures in her possession and she said she did not. I asked her if she had seen them and she hadn't seen them either. I had to be the one to break the bad news to her that she had just been scammed.

I know many actors today who started out in this business getting scammed. When you walk into an agency and your gut tells you to run, listen to your gut. Always listen to your gut. The gut always knows. Our business is full of wannabe actors. It seems that everyone wants to get into show business in one way or another. There are people out there who prey on those of you who are desperate to get into the business. There are modeling schools out there that also act as training grounds and then segue into the photography and the talent agency divisions as well.

One day, I was visiting one of these schools to see if they had any talent. I had been called and told that this school had some wonderful talent that I just had to see. I saw a girl walk in. She was in her late teens, about 5'2", very overweight, and she was, unfortunately, not very attractive. She walked in with her mother and what I observed just infuriated me. The director of the school greeted them warmly and started to tell this girl and her mother how she could make their dreams come true and turn this girl into a model. If this girl lived to be a hundred years old, she could not be turned into a model. She could, however, with proper training become a character actress. This was not why this mother brought her teenager into that modeling school, though. They filled these two heads full of promises that could never come true and then told them about a payment plan to extort, in my opinion, many hundreds of dollars from these people. Once I saw this, I walked out and never went back.

I wish I could shout from the rooftops and tell people not to let the words of these scam artists entice them when it involves very large sums of money. An agency does not charge you money to register with them. Should I repeat this? AN AGENCY DOES NOT CHARGE YOU MONEY TO REGISTER WITH THEM.

There are some extras casting companies that may charge you a nominal fee. It's a processing fee, but it should be less than $100.00 and you should be able to work out a deal if you can't afford it. Many companies like that will let you pay your processing fee out of your first job. This way, you can see if the company is going to get you work and then you can make sure you get paid. These extras companies also don't require that you spend many hundreds of dollars to get photos. A digital print, snapshot or Polaroid is sufficient to submit you for extra work. If an extras agency tells you otherwise, thank them very much and walk out.

It seems that every day another scam artist is opening up in town. They open up, take your money and close their doors just as fast. Don't be so anxious to plunk down many hundreds or thousands of dollars just to become an actor. There are many legitimate ways to get into this business and to make a career for yourself where you don't have to pay for it. Oftentimes, these so-called agencies will ask you to sign a contract. Don't sign anything without taking it to a lawyer to read. Also, don't freely give out your credit card number to pay for these very expensive classes and photos that you are being told you need. Once you get locked into a contract with someone, it may be very difficult to get out of it. Just keep your wits about you. Read everything before signing anything. Trust your gut and ask a lot of questions. If it seems too good to be true, it probably is.

Notes

Notes

12

Becoming Union:
SAG versus Non-SAG

A question I am often asked is how to become union. The union in question is Screen Actors Guild. SAG, as it is called, is the union that governs film and television. When an actor is filming a union commercial, film, or television project and they are in a union, it is SAG. There is another union called AFTRA. This stands for American Federation of Television and Radio Artists. It is possible to film a TV or film project under the AFTRA contract, but the difference is that AFTRA is recorded on tape and SAG is recorded on film. Soap operas and most sit-coms are filmed under the AFTRA contract. Most union films, commercials, and television shows are filmed under the SAG contract.

To become a SAG member—now read carefully—you have to book a SAG job. A SAG agent has to send you on a SAG casting in order to book a SAG project. Most SAG agents will not send an actor on a SAG project unless they are already a member of SAG. If you are not a member of SAG, and the only way to become a member is to book a SAG job, and your agent won't send you unless you are already a member, then how do you become a member?! This is quite a "Catch 22." When I give this explanation to people, they usually look at me like I'm crazy. It sounds really difficult to become a SAG member. Since there are many thousands of members, it can't be that difficult, now can it?

To become an AFTRA member, you just go to your local AFTRA office and plunk down your membership money and become a member. It's quite easy. The usual way to become a member of SAG is to book a SAG job. There are many ways to do this. The typical way would be to register with a SAG agent and get them to send you on a SAG casting. This can be a commercial, a TV show, a public service announcement, a film, or an industrial. It can be any film project that is signed to the SAG agreement. Once you are booked, your name is called into your local SAG office and then you can join. You can also join by shooting three SAG extra jobs on any SAG commercials. This makes you eligible to join. You may want to remain eligible until you absolutely have to join.

If your goal is to move to New York City or Los Angeles, our two biggest markets in this country, then you would want to have your SAG card before you go. Once you get there, it can be very difficult to obtain your SAG status. I know actors who have been out in Los Angeles for ten years or more and still can't get their SAG cards. If you want to move to one of the two biggest markets and you want your SAG card before moving, I have a really good suggestion. Investigate other markets and find out where there is a lot of filming going on. Move there for a while until you can obtain your SAG card before tackling a bigger market.

I am from the South Florida market. I can't tell you how many actors have walked through my doors and told me that they were only in Miami to get their SAG card before they moved on. The competition is far less in a smaller market. It is also a lot easier to get an agent to send you out on a SAG casting in a smaller market. Of course, there isn't as much work in a smaller market. That is why I strongly suggest that you do your homework and see which areas have a lot of filming. If your goal is to become union, then this is a good way to accomplish that goal.

Right now, there is a lot of filming in Louisiana, but this changes from year to year. There are many markets that go through the ups and downs. If you are in a right-to-work state, then you might not want to become union right away. A right-to-work state means that you can't be forced to join the union, but you still have the right to work on a union project. Many of these states have a lot of non-union work filmed there. Louisiana is a right-to-work state. They have a lot of union work being filmed there as well.

Non-union means you are not governed by any union. The good thing about this is that you don't have to join the union and give up your non-union status. The bad thing about this is that there are no union rules to protect you. The client can pay you anything they want. They can keep you as many hours as they can get away with and not pay overtime. They can feed you whatever, whenever. They can issue payment when they want. There are no time limits as to when that payment has to be made. They can run the commercial or air the film as many times as they want on any network and never pay you a penny more. No residuals for as long as that project airs.

Even if you are not a member of SAG, but you do shoot a SAG project, you are protected by all of the SAG rules. Any rule that applies to a SAG job has to apply to you, too. If you make enough money to qualify for SAG insurance, then you will be covered, regardless of whether you ever join SAG. This is a good thing. I know people who live and work in right-to-work states, who have been shooting SAG projects for years, but who have never joined. It is not necessary to join SAG when you live and work in a right-to-work state.

If you want to work in a state that is *not* right-to-work, such as New York or California, then you must be a member of SAG in good standing before you can work. A member in good standing means that your dues are all paid up and you don't have any fines against you. A union office will not let you work in a *non*-right-to-work state if you have any outstanding dues or debts.

It is definitely more professional and prestigious to be a SAG member, but it's not necessarily more lucrative. Many years ago a newer actress booked a part on a television show I was casting. She only wanted to be a member of SAG. I advised her against it, but she wanted that status on her résumé. I told her she should wait until she got her second SAG job before joining, but she wanted to join right away. It took her four more years from that point before she booked another SAG job.

If you are non-union and auditioning for union roles, your competition will have a lot more experience than you. This is why I say you may want to wait before joining SAG. This will not prohibit you from auditioning again for another SAG job, but it will also allow you to keep auditioning for non-union work as well. At this juncture, you have the best of both worlds. You are eligible for both union and non-union work. Once you book your second union job, then you can go ahead and join if you want.

Another way you can become eligible to join is by being upgraded on a film or television project. I hear so often that people don't want to do extra work on a movie or a TV show. The pay is low and the prestige is nothing. I do, however, know many people who have been working on a SAG set as an extra and have been plucked out of the crowd and given a line of dialogue. All you have to do is say one word, utter one sound, even a scream from your mouth on a TV or film shoot, and you become eligible for a SAG contract.

On a commercial, it is a bit different. You don't necessarily have to speak, but you have to be recognizable in the foreground for three seconds. You can be recognizable in the foreground for three minutes in a TV or film project but unless you utter sound from your mouth, you are not eligible to join SAG.

Make sure you know all of your rules and regulations on how to become SAG when you are on a SAG shoot. If you are in a commercial and you even think you may be a principal, call your local SAG office and have them look at the commercial to determine if you indeed deserve an upgrade.

I cast a national spot many years ago, after which the mother of the little girl in the spot called to say that she thought her daughter might be a principal. I suggested that she call the union office to have them review the footage. She dragged her feet and never got around to it. When the commercial was done airing, she finally called the union. They reviewed it and determined that she was indeed a principal. It was too late by that point. We figured out that she lost about $12,000.00 by not checking it out right away.

Clients will most likely not come forward to offer you these sums of money, so you have to be on top of it yourself. If you are working as an extra on a SAG commercial and you want to join SAG, it is imperative that you stay on top of the finished product to make sure you have not been upgraded. Sometimes you will hear a client say that they'll determine if you are a principal once they edit all of the footage together. Let me tell you something—if you are filmed as a principal, then you are a principal regardless of whether they edit you in or out. If you want to be a member of SAG and you believe you are being filmed as a principal, you must make sure you get a SAG contract before you leave the set.

There are so many films shot with well-known actors, and when it comes time to edit the film, those actors may be edited out because, for one reason or another, the part just doesn't seem to work. These actors are paid as principals. They are not told that they won't get paid if they are edited out. You should be treated the same way.

Another wonderful way to get a SAG part is to ask for one. Ask for one?! Yes! I was casting a television series once, when an actress asked if I would read her for any part, she wasn't picky. She just needed her SAG card before she moved to New York. All she needed was to say a word, a scream, a cough, something audible. She called me once a week, just to remind me. That's all you need to do: Call, remind me who you are, say, "I want to be SAG. Thank you. Goodbye." Don't engage any of us in a long conversation. Postcards work as well. You can drop somebody a postcard with your picture on it. Make sure your phone number is on it. Write, "Please, please, please, don't forget me. I want to become a member of SAG."

I was casting for a small part of a secretary and I brought in the actress who had called me every week. She booked it. Please, remember, where there is a will, there is a way. If you truly have the desire to become SAG, then you can accomplish it. Make sure you associate with the appropriate people who can give you the opportunities to become SAG and stay with them.

There is also something called *Financial Core*. Financial Core means you have been a member of Screen Actors Guild and you want to be eligible to work in the non-union market again, but you don't want to relinquish the opportunity to continue doing SAG work. Financial Core basically means you give up your full SAG status. You become a dues-paying non-member. You lose the right to vote in SAG elections and you lose the right to attend Screen Actors Guild membership meetings. You maintain all of the other rights and privileges that a SAG member has. Many people join SAG and then immediately file for Financial Core status, so they are eligible to do both SAG and non-union work. If you are going to be staying in a right-to-work state, then you don't necessarily need to be a member of Screen Actors Guild, but if you are going to work in New York or California, then it is important for you to be a member of Screen Actors Guild. You need to review all of your options and determine if joining SAG is the right choice for you.

Notes

13
The Most Important Person

Who is the most important person in any office? The *secretary,* of course! Most people do not recognize that. The secretary person answers the phone, opens the mail, passes the messages on to the boss, or not. This person is the link to getting to the boss. If you don't get past the secretary, you don't move forward.

When I was casting *Miami Vice,* my assistant was also my little sister, Marjorie. If you have a little sister, you know you are very protective over this person. If anyone hurts her, isn't nice to her, disrespects her in any way, you will fiercely defend your sister to the end. So, there I was, casting *Miami Vice,* and actors from all over the world were clamoring to get to me. If you didn't get past Marjorie, you didn't get to me. There was an actor who was trying to get a read for the series and he had been schmoozing my assistant. When a part came up that he was right for, my sister asked me to please read him (said in a whining voice that only sisters can get away with). I brought him in to read. He wasn't a member of the union. He didn't have any TV or film credits either, but I read him because my sister had asked. Lo and behold, he happened to be a great actor and he booked a really substantial role.

This can work the other way as well. Many years ago, I had an assistant named Ken. He was wonderful, my right hand for sure. He and I were the only two people who worked in my office at that time. During the holiday season, he happened to be alone in the office when an actress came in with a holiday gift for me. It was the comedy and tragedy masks, made out of white and milk chocolate. She had made them herself, she pronounced. They looked beautiful. She handed them to Ken to give to me. She made a big deal out of them and asked him to make sure that he gave them to me. On her way out the door, she looked back at Ken and said, "Don't forget me now."

Of course, Ken never did forget her, but not in the way she had wanted. How hard would it have been for her to make two sets of these masks or to just box them individually, giving us each one mask? Not very. In slighting him, she hurt his feelings, and in turn, hurt mine.

Most talent agencies and casting offices around the country employ minimal staff. Even if you are dealing with some of the giant agencies, you'll still have a very small circle of people with whom you would deal. There is the person who answers the phone, the assistant to your specific agent, and maybe one or two others. It is imperative that you acknowledge all of them when you walk in with a little something, such as: "Thank you," or "Happy Holidays." And you do want to send or bring in a little something for everyone to say, "Thank you," or "Happy Holidays."

I have a wonderful story that I love to tell. I was on one of my business trips to Los Angeles and I really wanted to get in to see the head of casting at one of the biggest networks. I called and Reggie answered the phone. I talked to her and practically begged her to let me speak to her boss. I knew if I didn't get past her, I'd never speak to the head honcho. She liked me and she forwarded me on to her boss. This was a wonderful thing.

Another consideration that you must take into account is that sometimes we, the casting directors, answer our own phones. I can't tell you how many times I've answered my own phone when the office gets busy. I have also called many of my talent agent and casting director friends who also answered their own phones. It is amazing how often I hear attitude from an actor who thinks they are just talking to the lowly secretary, and then, when they think I've picked up the phone, I hear the tone change in their voice. There is a condescending tone in their voice when talking to the underling, but when speaking to me, they are much nicer. This tells me a lot about their character. When I first started in this business, I was the secretary at the front desk of the largest talent agency in South Florida. There were three of us working in this office: the two owner/talent agents, and I. I did everything. I answered the phones. I watered the plants. I made the coffee. I opened the mail. I saw the pictures or I didn't. I wrote out the checks. I called the talent for castings. I suggested actors to clients. I videotaped actors for exclusive clients and so on. I was the first person there in the morning and the last person to leave at night. I checked the answering machine in the morning and updated the owners on everything that was going on. I was the everything.

One day, after I had been working at this position for about two years, an actor walked into the office. My two bosses were out to lunch. By this point, I was a sub-agent and I was definitely the go-to person in this office, which was still just the three of us. This actor asked to see either of my bosses. I informed him that they were out and that maybe I could help him. He could not have been ruder to me. He informed me that he didn't want to talk to me, that he wanted to talk to "someone who knew something around here." I told him I knew a thing or two and he continued to insist on talking to someone "in there," as he pointed to the other room where the two owners had their office.

I could not believe his audacity. I got up from my desk and walked into their office and shouted from the other room, "I'm in here now! Do you want to talk to me?" I then walked back to the front and explained that he had two choices: He could either talk to me or he could leave. He said he didn't know me and I told him I didn't know him either! He was from South Florida originally, but had been living in L.A. and hadn't been back in town since I started working at the agency. This actor still lives in South Florida and I have gone from being a secretary at the front desk of an agency to one of the most prominent casting directors in the Southeast. You just never know where the *lowly secretary* will end up.

Before another L.A. excursion, I wanted to make an appointment to meet the head of casting at one of the major studios. I have always known that the secretary is the most important person. I called up and a girl named Victoria answered the phone. Victoria was very sweet and nice, but the head of casting for this major studio didn't want to talk to me. So, I talked to Victoria, because she knew this man. I asked her all about him. Then I asked, "Should I write him a letter?" She said, "Yes, I think that's a great idea. I think you should write him a letter." I said, "Wow, great idea, Victoria. I'll take your advice." Even though it was my idea in the first place, I made it her advice and I made it her idea. Once I made it her idea, she was feeling proud. After sending her the correspondence, then calling her back, she got me in to see the head of casting for this major studio. Please, know how important the secretary or assistant is in any office and make them feel so.

I have worked with many huge casting directors in Los Angeles and New York who started as the assistants to big casting directors before they broke out on their own. We all have to start somewhere and it's nice to know that the casting director has worked his way up the ranks so he has a better understanding of the position. The main point of this section is: Treat everyone with equal respect and sometimes the secretary gets a bit more. They are the backbone of the office. They often know the comings and goings of the office better than the boss. They are the constant. They are the one who will get you in the door or not. Put yourself in their position and see how you would feel if you were left out. "Do unto others," as it is written.

Notes

14
Extras and Such

You know, you always hear that you shouldn't do extra work. It's beneath you. "If you ever want to become a star or a worthwhile working actor, you shouldn't do extra work." You've heard that, right? Well, I am going to disagree with that. I have a list of stars who did extra work when they first started out in this business. It's not a crime. There's nothing wrong with it. You have to start somewhere, and if you do extra work, you will learn so much.

What is an extra? This is a person in the background of the film or television project. They do not speak, you may not even see their face fully, but they are an essential component of the shoot. Picture a scene on a beach during Spring break. Do you have that visual in your mind? Now, picture it without the extras. The extras are all of the beachgoers, sunbathers, swimmers, beach volleyball players, and so on. What would that beach look like if there were no extras? It would be a very different atmosphere, wouldn't it?

Being on a set, you will learn all of the verbal jargon that is necessary to know when you're filming. You will have to understand this jargon when filming. If you are on a set and they tell you to go "back to one," or go back to where you started when the shooting began, and you have no idea what that means, then you will stand there and potentially get yourself in trouble. There is no class to take that will teach you these terms. What better way is there to learn than when you're on a set? You will even get some payment for your efforts, albeit small, but it's better than nothing. If you have never been on a set before, this is a wonderful learning experience. If you can get some work as a stand-in or a photo-double, that can be an even greater learning experience.

A stand-in, because I'm sure you're wondering what I'm talking about, is someone who stands in for the principal actor while the crew is lighting or blocking the scenes. The principal might be getting their makeup done, getting dressed, working on their dialogue, or preparing themselves in some way while the crew is getting the set ready for the actual shoot.

A photo-double is someone who looks like the principal actor and is the same height, weight, size and coloring. This person is actually filmed as the main actor. Usually, this person is being filmed from the back, the side or just a portion of their body, at a distance. The reason a photo-double is used is because the main actor is not available to be on the set at that time. There are many reasons that actor cannot be on the set, but the photo-double insures that the filming can continue and the production won't lose any time. I have known stand-ins and photo-doubles for many high profile actors who will actually travel with that actor to do all of their on-location shoots.

A friend of mine admired a very well-known, Oscar-winning actor and he looked a lot like him. He had heard that this actor was doing a movie in his area. He found out who was in charge of hiring the stand-ins and made sure he got seen for that particular part. He booked it and from that point on, he became this actor's stand-in whenever and wherever he shot in the United States. A stand-in or photo-double role is not usually considered a Screen Actors Guild role. This actor wanted to make sure his stand-in was well taken care of, so he arranged to have a SAG weekly contract available every time they worked together. I have done films with numerous name actors, and many of them travel with their own stand-ins and photo-doubles. The same person doubles as both, many times, so they will find a stand-in who looks enough like them, who has the same size, same height, same coloring, so they can act as their photo-double as well. The contacts you make working with these stars are invaluable, and you are earning a living by working in an industry that you love.

I know I'm making it sound so easy by telling you to just go and become an extra or go and become a stand-in or photo-double, but it really is not as hard as you think. There are extras companies in various cities all over the country. As I have suggested before, call your local film office and find out which projects are currently filming in your area. Contact the casting director. They should be able to steer you in the direction of the extras casting person.

There are many different kinds of extra work out there. The movie, *Forrest Gump*, for example, has hundreds of actors clumped together, milling about at a distance where you can't make any of them out. Then, there might be a scene like the one I cast in *Wild Things* where I needed a waitress, an extra, who was serving lunch to the characters being played by Bill Murray and Robert Wagner—only one featured extra. She was still considered an extra, but there were only three people in the scene and the other two were the stars of the movie. You can pick and choose the extra work you want to do, but if you are just starting out, it is a wonderful way to learn and get recognized by the local casting people. You can network with the other extras and possibly meet the executives on the set.

There was a TV show starring a very good looking male star. A young lady worked as an extra one day and caught the eye of the male star. He went over to talk to her, and, as they say, the rest was history. Yes, indeed, they ended up getting married. So, you never know who you are going to meet on a set.

If you are on a set, you have to believe that you are going to meet other people who work on sets as well. You will not only meet other extras, you will meet the actors, crew types, producers and directors. If you don't put yourself out there, then you will have no chance of learning or being seen. This business is all about networking. You cannot sit in your home, staring at the phone, waiting for it to ring. You have to make things happen. If you are just starting out in this acting business or even if you've been in this business awhile, you need to get credits for your résumé. Working as an extra is a wonderful stepping stone to bigger and better things.

Working as an extra on a commercial can also be a very lucrative project. Many years ago, I brought an actor in to audition for a commercial that I was casting. I asked him, "If you're not chosen as a principal, would you work as an extra?" His answer to me was, "Definitely." He said, "Many years ago, I said no. I thought I was better than that, and they chose somebody else. That somebody else got upgraded and the commercial ran for an extended period of time and that actor made $17,000.00." So, I say to you, as this actor said to me, "I will never turn down a SAG extra role on a commercial again."

I was casting another commercial and I needed twelve SAG extras. SAG extras make a few hundred dollars. It's a decent day's pay, right? These extras started working at 6:00 in the morning and they worked until 2:00 the next morning. That's a lot of overtime. They didn't finish, so they had to be brought back the next night to finish. There was not only overtime, there were meal penalties, and a night premium. When all was said and done, each one of these extras made $3,000.00 for their work on this commercial for twenty-four hours. Keep in mind, extra work can be very lucrative and there are actors out there who make their living doing just extra work. Extra work can be a wonderful stepping stone and can add credits to your résumé until you start booking the principal roles.

Notes

15
Getting the Call

When the call for the casting comes in, you must be ready. You have to know what to ask, why and how. Here's how this process works. Your agent calls you and says, "I have a casting for you." You need to know what the casting is for. "We want you to audition for a television show." Where is the casting? "At Lori Wyman Casting." OK, you want to make sure Lori Wyman Casting hasn't moved. That has happened where actors are unaware that a casting facility has moved, so they go to the wrong place and are late. Of course, if it's at a place that you go to on a frequent basis, you will know where they are.

Let's talk about the character for which you are auditioning. Maybe you are auditioning for a high-powered attorney. Great! Now you want to find out a little more information about this high-powered attorney. What might you wear? You might wear a business suit. Then you come to find out that this high-powered attorney is on a boat. Oh! On the yacht of one of her wealthiest clients. That might change things. So, maybe you're wearing a pair of slacks, a nice Polo shirt and a blazer. Then you come to find out that you and your biggest client are the only two people on this yacht and you're having an affair with the client. Now what do you wear on this audition? Do you see how things change? That is why you need to have questions answered before you hang up from your agent.

Is there dialogue? Can you get the dialogue? How do you get the dialogue, or *sides*, as dialogue pages are called. As I speak about in the morsel on sides, there are several different ways to obtain sides. They can be faxed to you or emailed. You can download them off of various sites that have sides. However it is that you can get these sides, you must get them before your audition.

You want to know when it shoots. It sounds pretty simple, but you must know when it shoots, because guess what? If you are not available for the shoot, then that's the end of the conversation and you don't go on the audition at all. I cannot tell you how many actors have come into my office and when I tell them when it shoots, they say, "Oh, but I'm not going to be here." And, I have to say, "OK, goodbye." Don't waste your time, or anybody else's. I was talking to an actor friend of mine who makes his living as an actor. He told me he was going on an audition and I asked him, "When does it shoot?" he said, "I don't know." I said, "Didn't you ask?" He said, "No, I guess it doesn't matter." I reminded him that it did matter, because he was already booked on another movie the following month for several weeks. I asked, "Why waste your time if you are not available for the shoot?" That's exactly what happened. He went on the casting. He booked the second job and then he wasn't able to do it, because he wasn't available for the shoot. Casting directors aren't too happy when an actor comes in to read for a role and then is not available. It's really important that you have all of your information up front before you go on an audition.

When you get the call, you must always have paper and something to write with at your disposal. Keep it in your car. Keep it next to your phone in your house. Don't start taking information, get halfway through the conversation, then say to your agent, "Oh, wait a minute. I should be writing this down." You should be writing it down from the very beginning of that conversation.

If this is a union job, then union scale is set at a certain rate. If this is a non-union job, then it is important for you to find out what the rate is. Many non-union jobs pay very well. Many union jobs, especially many union films, may be under a SAG low-budget agreement. Some of the SAG low-budget agreements pay as little as $100.00 per day. Maybe you think $100.00 per day is a low rate to work for, but you want to obtain footage for your demo reel. Possibly you want the experience, you want the exposure, or you want to do this because you find out there might be a celebrity in this movie. I recently cast a non-union movie. The pay was $100.00 a day. It was very low budget. Several of the actors were happy to work on it. Why? It turned out that after the movie was completed, one of the stars of the movie went on to book a major television series. This actress is in commercials for huge makeup companies. She's in the news every week. She also does print ads and billboards. The series that she is in, at this writing, has been airing for several years and is an EMMY winning television show. She started in this little non-union, low-budget movie. You never know who is going to be in these movies. You just never know whom you are going to meet, so I strongly suggest that you don't turn it down unless your schedule doesn't allow it.

There are certain specifications that a casting director will ask for and this will be conveyed to the agent. You want the agent to pass this information on to you, the actor. For instance, they might want you to bring three headshots to the casting. The reason for this is because they may be dealing with three different clients for the same project who are in three different locations. A good way to make sure you don't forget these is to keep a supply of headshots and résumés in your car at all times. That way you won't be caught short at the casting.

The bottom line is that once you get the call, it is imperative to find out every piece of information that you can in order to be as prepared as possible to go on your casting.

Notes

Notes

16
Sides

What are sides? Sides are that portion of the script that has your particular character on it. If a script is one hundred pages long, we, as casting directors, go through the script and pull out the pages that have your character on them—the character for which you are auditioning. We will mark those sides and get them to you. Sides may be one page, ten pages, twenty pages. There is no limit to how short or long they can be. It all depends on how many pages your character is on. We just need to see enough of your audition to make a determination as to whether you are right or not right for the part.

How do we mark them? We will put the name of the character for which you're auditioning at the top or along the side margin of the page. Then we will see how many total pages these sides actually are. If there are seven pages, for instance, I will, as do many casting directors, put "1 of 7," "2 of 7," "3 of 7," and so on until we get to "7 of 7." This is a big clue. Pay attention here. This tells you how many pages you should have, as well as in what order they should be read.

It is unbelievable to me how many actors will receive their sides and see that there should be seven pages. They have only received six of these seven pages and yet they do not call their agent to find out where the last page is! The actor will then come into my office and I will ask them if they have any questions. They will say, no, they don't. We will begin to rehearse the dialogue and they will stop before the actual end of the sides. When I ask them why they don't continue, they tell me that's all they have. When I ask them if they saw that there was a total of seven pages and they finished at six, I usually get the very same response, which goes something like this: "Yeah, I wondered about that." Why they didn't think to ask their agent or ask my office when they first arrived for their casting is beyond me. That has occurred on more than one occasion and it boggles the mind.

Are you ready for this one? I was casting a series regular on a TV show. There were twelve audition pages for the actor to learn. Apparently the pages arrived in his fax machine exactly backwards, so he received page number twelve first, then eleven, then ten, and so on. The top of each page read like this, "12 of 12," "11 of 12," "10 of 12," "9 of 12," etc. The actual page numbers were typewritten on the script, so even if he did receive twelve pages of dialogue backwards, the actual script page numbers should have told him in what order to learn his lines.

If he had looked at these actual typewritten pages, he would have seen the correct order of the script. Not to mention that the order of the sides was also written in dark marker at the top of each page. When he came in to audition as a series regular for this TV show, a role that would last six weeks at $10,000.00 per week, he had memorized all twelve pages, which was wonderful. Unfortunately, he had memorized all twelve pages backwards. In my casting room, when he began on page twelve, I asked him to start at the beginning. He said he *was* at the beginning. I could not believe that he actually worked on this amount of pages, memorized them, and didn't realize that the dialogue wasn't flowing. It was also unbelievable that at some point while working on this dialogue, he never thought to glance at either my hand-written page numbers or the scripted page numbers.

There will also be another set of numbers known as the scene numbers. The scene numbers do not necessarily correspond with the actual page numbers. The only time they are exactly the same is when you have page one, scene one. After that, there is no guarantee that the page numbers and the scene numbers will be the same.

You know, it's funny, there was an actor who had taken my seminar a number of times and when I told that story about the actor who memorized twelve pages backwards, he always laughed. He thought that was so funny. Everybody who hears my lecture laughs. How can somebody pick twelve pages up and memorize them backwards? Didn't they realize? Sounds rather ridiculous, right? This actor, after taking my class many times, went out to Los Angeles all nervous and excited. He got an audition for a starring role in a feature film. The pages were faxed to his hotel, however, the pages were faxed backwards and the front desk stapled them that way. Even though he had heard my story a number of times, he memorized the pages the way they were given to him—backwards!

He even worked over the phone with a coach, who said, "Something doesn't sound right." The actor said, "No, no, no. This is how it should be." When he went into the actual audition, the casting director looked at him and said, "But you're doing the sides backwards."

Please, pay attention to what you have just read! Make sure you look at the page numbers, either in the upper right hand corner or along the side margin of your sides, to make sure you are actually memorizing your dialogue in the correct order.

When you get these sides, you must first read the entire set of sides out loud. This means you must read your lines out loud, the other person's lines, and all of the direction in between. This is so you get to know the flow of the sides. You have to know what your cue lines are in order to respond properly. You also want to know what the other person is saying, so that you can acknowledge them with possible nodding, smiling, pointing or any other gesture that seems appropriate at the time. When reading these sides, you want to look for clues as to where and when the scene takes place. You will see *int* or *ext*, which indicates whether the scene takes place in the interior or exterior. Does it say *day* or *night* or *dawn* or *dusk*?

PLEASE REMEMBER: These are mini scenes. There is a beginning, middle, and end. You have to create this scene using the sides you have. DON'T FORGET THIS. It is so important. This set of audition sides was not written as an audition piece. It was written as part of a script. We then pluck these pages out and tell you to make an audition out of them. You must make them come to life. You have to make them as real and as natural as possible, using the surroundings at your disposal. If your dialogue is supposed to take place in a swimming pool, create the illusion that you're in a swimming pool, just coming out of the pool, or just going into the pool. Maybe you dress in a bathing suit and bring a beach towel and act as if you're drying off while you're reciting your dialogue. Chances are there will not be a swimming pool at your audition. Keep this in mind. You have to create the illusion. We have to sense the presence of the swimming pool in your audition.

I had a set of sides once where the first line of dialogue was actually a gesture. The actor was supposed to extend his hand in which he held a small bugging device. He needed to show something to the other actor to give him the incentive to say, "Where was that?" If you don't show the reader the item, then it doesn't make sense for her to start the scene by saying, "Where was that?" If the reader does give you that cue line, but you haven't shown her the item, it looks rather awkward.

During another casting session, I had the first line, which was, "What is your name?" The actor stopped right there and apologized for not introducing himself upon walking into the room. This faux-pas could have been easily avoided if only the actor had read the entire set of sides and known what the first line was supposed to be. This mistake happens more than you know. I cannot impress upon you enough that when you get your sides, you read everything. Read your lines. Read the other person's lines and read all the direction in between. Did I say this before? Well, I'm saying it again. To do your audition properly, make sure you know every single word on that page.

Don't, however, read any lines out loud on an audition except your own. You should not read the direction out loud, either. Let me tell you why I mention that.

My modus operandi is that I rehearse the dialogue with the actor before we record it. This is what I do. Many casting directors don't do that. You don't have the opportunity to review before you actually are put on tape. I like to do that before I record it. It just helps loosen up the actor and in case there are any mistakes, I can catch them before I actually hit record on the camera. I want to make sure that the actor has the correct pages. I also want to make sure that the actor knows how to pronounce everything and that the audition can be the very best it can be before I start the camera. Every casting director is not like that, so you have to make sure that you have everything lined up before you go into that audition session. I especially like to pre-read an actor before I bring him in to meet the director.

Once I had a callback session on a series and didn't have time to pre-screen a particular actor. The agent assured me that he was good and that I would not be embarrassed. We were in such a time crunch that I took the agent's word. This actor arrived and I brought him directly in to meet the director and producer. The actor's character was that of a police officer who was having a shootout with a criminal. He recited his line and then said, "The police officer runs for cover as the bullets whiz by his head." When he said this out loud, I was so embarrassed. That was the direction in between the dialogue! It is *never* said out loud by the actor. You see, this actor had been a theater actor and while he knew how to act, he knew nothing about auditioning for TV or film. Needless to say, he did not get the part, but that could have been avoided if he had only known how to audition for film and television.

Auditioning for theater is completely different from auditioning for film and television. Speaking of auditioning for a television series, if you are auditioning for a TV series that is on the air at the time of your audition, I strongly suggest that you watch an episode or two to understand the kind of acting that is done. It may be an understated type of acting, over the top, quirky, or comedic. It is really important that you are in keeping with that style of acting. It's also important to know the names of all the players in that series and who they are. This way, you will know to whom you are speaking and what their position is in the show.

I mention this because when I was casting the TV show, *Miami Vice*, I had this happen to me: An actor came in to audition for a day player. A day player is just that, an actor who will work a day or two. The character is not a series regular, a recurring part, or a guest star.

As we started to rehearse, this actor started to read the Crockett lines. I asked him why he was doing that. I told him he was supposed to read for Cop #1. Even though his character was written at the top of the page, which is where the character you're reading for is written, he told me that he decided to read for the Crockett character, because he liked it better and it was a bigger part. I explained to him that Crockett had already been cast and I didn't think that Don Johnson would want to give up his part at that time to this actor.

All of these actors mentioned above were at their audition, but weren't really ready. Let's go back to the page numbers and scene numbers for a minute. It is important that you know what page and/or scene number you're supposed to prepare for your audition. I had told an actor I was auditioning to prepare scene #52. He arrived at the audition and when I asked him if he had any questions, he informed me that he was given the wrong pages. I told him he was supposed to be given scene #52. Yes, but he had received pages 36 and 37. I told him that was correct, that *scene #52* was on *pages* 36 and 37. This poor actor did not know the difference between page numbers and scene numbers, so he had not prepared his sides. It was his turn to audition and he didn't know his dialog.

I do a lot of what are referred to as *searches* in Florida. A *search* is when a production is looking to cast a specific role but they can't seem to find the right actor in their particular area. They contact me in Florida and ask me to look in my talent pool to see if I can cast that role for them. Since these are bigger roles, I like to give the sides out far enough in advance that the actor can really learn them. If you are being given sides in advance for a major role, I strongly suggest you invest the time and effort to learn these sides. It's really important. I can't stress this enough.

According to Screen Actors Guild, as I've said before, "The script shall be made available to performers at the casting office no later than twenty-four hours prior to their audition." Most casting directors will prepare the actual audition sides for you, so you can concentrate on exactly what you need to know. Get those sides! It is imperative to block out the time and work on your dialog if you hope to book this. It is your agent's responsibility to make sure you get those sides, but ultimately, it is your responsibility. Even if those sides are faxed or emailed, you still need to learn them. You still need to get them and you still need to work on them. The agent works for you, as I've said before, but you know the old saying, "You can lead a horse to water," so just because we get those sides to you, doesn't insure that you will know them. What will insure that you know them is you! Today's modern technology makes it easy to get those sides to you, but you're the one who has to do the work. Do not go into an audition without getting those sides in advance and knowing them.

It's OK for you to hold your sides on an audition. There is no crime in this. If you don't need them, that would be better. It is better to hold the sides and not need them than to not hold the sides and need them. An actor came to a session in front of the producer and director. This actor was determined not to hold his sides, but he didn't know them as well as he should have. He began his dialogue and forgot his line. The producer, who was quite nice, told him to hold the sides, but the actor didn't want to. The actor started over, again and again, but forgot his line at the very same place each time. Again, the producer told him to hold the sides. This happened three times until I emphatically told the actor to hold the sides! By this time, the producer was a bit miffed and the actor lost the attention of everyone in the room. Please, remember, if you need to hold the sides, go ahead and hold them. It may just be a security blanket for you and that's just fine.

I knew an actor who was always memorized, but would always hold the sides, just in case. Feel free to do the same. Sides are a very important tool for you to get the job. If you don't get them in advance and don't know what to do with them once you get them, then you will not get booked. They are the first step in this process, so make sure you pay special attention to them. Spend as many hours as necessary in order to perfect them before going into your audition.

While you are working on the sides, make sure you go over and over and over the dialogue out loud, out loud, out loud. I have a very good friend who makes his living as an actor. When I visit him and he has an audition, he works on his dialogue incessantly. He tells me that he works on his dialog in the shower, while getting dressed and in the car. Even when he is out to dinner with friends, he'll launch into his dialogue out loud. It's important! If this is something that you intend to do, if this is something you want to pursue as your career, then working on the sides, knowing the sides and doing them over and over and over is imperative. The more you put into it, the more you will get out of it.

Notes

17

To Memorize or Not to Memorize

Every time I teach a class, I tell the class that I think they should be memorized before they go into an audition. Somebody always raises his hand to disagree with me. Then I have to go through this whole barrage of examples to prove my point. I usually dance around the room, holding sides, showing the class the difference between holding the sides and not holding the sides. I will attempt to create a visual image for you to prove that my view is the correct one.

Picture, if you will, that you are doing a scene between two people. You are the only one who is auditioning and you need to hold your sides because you are not completely memorized. This is a pretty intense scene, in which you yell at and threaten someone. You also hold your sides, since you are not memorized, remember? You begin your dialogue. You look right into the other character's eyes, or in the case of an audition, you look directly into the lens of the camera. With great intensity, you say, "If I ever catch you with my boyfriend again, I'm going to rip you right out of your chair, take you outside, throw you up against the big oak tree out back and . . . and . . ." Oops! You have to look down, because you aren't completely memorized and you just can't remember that last line. This serves to distract whoever is watching, not to mention, it throws you off completely. You have to be in the moment and if you have to interrupt your dialogue delivery by looking down at your sides, then you are not doing your job properly.

During one particular casting, I had a waiting room full of actors. I like it quiet out in the waiting room, as noise can distract the actor who is auditioning, not to mention the actors preparing to audition. It also disturbs my sense of concentration. I kept hearing the same male voice out in the waiting room. I went out to ask the room to please hold it down and then went back to continue my audition. The noise level rose again, with this same male voice rising above all other voices. Again, I went to shush the room. After the third time, I asked this actor, whom I had never seen before, if he knew his dialogue. His response to me was, "It's only two lines." Since I didn't know this actor, I didn't know the caliber of his talent, so maybe only two lines was really not a big deal to him. It was now his turn. This actor walked into my room and immediately informed me that he was from New York. I asked him if he had any questions and he said he didn't. OK, I begin. I read my first line and he stopped and looked down at his line. I wondered why he looked down and I asked him, "Aren't you memorized?" When I inquired as to what he had been doing in the waiting room for the past twenty minutes with "only two lines," he told me that no one had told him he should memorize it. "Anyway, he proclaimed, he was much better than two lines." Out he went, never even finishing those two little lines.

You see, when you come into a casting, you're probably a little nervous. If you are alive, you are a little nervous. Many years ago, a good friend of mine was performing in a play on Broadway. He had actually won a Tony Award for his role. He performed eight shows a week. You would have figured that he knew his dialogue backwards and forwards. He confessed to me that he got butterflies before each and every performance. You have to figure that if a Tony Award winner, who is doing eight shows a week on Broadway, gets butterflies before each performance, then an actor who doesn't audition every week, let alone every day, is going to have a bit of the jitters before his casting, too. The better you know your dialogue, the easier that audition will be for you. If you don't know your dialogue, you'll have to keep looking down. Add in the nervous factor and your audition could be seriously doomed.

Think of an audition as a mid-term exam. Do you remember when you were back in school and you had a big test? If you had studied really hard and you knew that material backwards and forwards, you would come into the class, sit down and just breeze through the test. What if you hadn't really studied hard? What if you had gotten up at 4:00 that morning and crammed for a few hours and then rushed in to class? Do you remember taking *those* tests? I do. I would sit at my desk and stare at the test, wondering when an answer would come to me. Then I watched the other students walk to the front of the room, confidently turning in their papers, shooting the class a broad grin as they smugly walked out of the classroom. Auditioning is the same principle. If you know your dialogue up and down, back and forth, you'll walk in to that casting and ace that audition.

How does one memorize? There are many ways to do it. My answer to you is whatever works for you is the best way. I have found that repetition out loud is the best way. You have to do it out loud. You cannot do it in your head. Think of your dialogue as a song. Would you practice a song in your head without ever having heard it come out of your mouth? Can you imagine looking at words to a song and singing it for the very first time out loud when you are on stage? I cannot tell you how many times an actor has come into my casting room and we begin to do the dialogue. A word comes out of their mouth and you can see a surprised look on their face. I ask them if they have ever heard this word before. The answer is usually *no*. The first time you hear a particular word come out of your mouth should not be when you are performing it in front of the casting director or the client. The first time you hear those words better be when you recite them out loud BEFORE your audition.

You want to loosen up your mouth, your tongue, your face. You want to say these words in the mirror, in the car, in your living room, the bathroom, the street, the closet. You want to say these words everywhere and anywhere you can before you have to go in for your audition. Before dinner, after dinner, before you go to bed and right when you wake up. You want to say these words out loud every chance you get so that they become yours. You want them to become a part of you so that the body starts to join in. Maybe your arm does something when you say a certain line, or your hand makes a gesture or your torso turns. It doesn't matter what happens, but you have to make these words your own. They have to fit like a glove. You see, if you don't do this before you go on a casting, then someone else will and they will be the person who books this job. It's that plain and simple.

If you are not good at memorizing, then take a memorization course. Many classes offered out there may not be specifically geared for actors, but a memorization class would certainly complement an actor's needs. You have probably seen one of those late-night infomercials that show some guy sitting on a stage in front of three hundred people he has never seen before, and he can miraculously recite each and every name after hearing it only once. This is because he took this remarkable memorization course. That's the course you want to take. When I tell you that whatever works for you is what you need to use in order to learn how to memorize, that is what I mean.

Getting involved in a play might also be helpful. If you have never done a play and you are not a member of Actors Equity Association, the union that governs theater, then get involved in community theater. You need to practice memorization on a daily basis. You have heard the saying, "Practice makes perfect." Well, that is definitely the case when learning how to memorize dialogue. Look at your local newspaper and find the section on auditions. You will see casting calls for local community theater. You may also want to contact your local houses of worship and see if they have any shows that are getting ready to cast. It is important to get out there and get involved with projects where your memorization skills are being challenged.

This exercise may sound utterly boring, but it will work: Pick up a newspaper or a magazine and start memorizing text. Yes, I know this sounds mundane, but if you are not good at memorizing, then you have to work at it. Just start getting in the habit of memorizing. You can also go to the local library or a bookstore and get books of scripts or monologues. Memorize them. Keep training your brain to memorize. If you practice this skill on a daily basis, then when you get the audition script, you can easily pick it up and work on it. This way the memorizing will not be a problem and you can concentrate on the acting.

Some acting coaches might tell you that you shouldn't memorize your sides before an audition. You may hear this because they don't want you to be so rigid that you wouldn't be able to change something if the director wanted you to.

I believe you must memorize your sides in order to be flexible enough to shift the performance any way the director asks. You will see. Go into the audition and be one hundred percent prepared and then you have done everything you can. The rest will be out of your hands. You must always be memorized. I don't care what anyone says, you must always be memorized. That is something I stand by one hundred percent.

Notes

Notes

18
Dress the Part

I have mentioned this topic in another morsel, but I believe it is important enough to deserve its own morsel. When I say, "Dress the part," I don't mean that you should come in looking like you are wearing a Halloween costume. I mean you should give the illusion that you are whom you are trying to portray. Just the other day I was casting a project and I needed a dad. This dad was supposed to be a very wealthy dad who was raising his sixteen-year-old daughter by himself after his wife died. His dialogue stated how conservative he was and how strict he was with her, regarding her music, attire and friends. He was clearly wealthy, refined, and educated. The first actor who came in was wearing an earring, had his hair cut in a very trendy manner and was wearing jeans and a t-shirt. Right away, I looked at him and thought, he doesn't really fit the part, but I want to give him a chance to do his audition. Another actor came in with rumpled khaki pants, a plaid work shirt and sneakers. This was not in keeping with the idea of this character either. The gentleman who booked the part had on a pair of slacks and a button-down, long sleeve shirt. His hair was cut short, in a conservative style. He had no facial hair. I am not saying that this and only this will get you the part, but if you look like what they envision, it will certainly grab the client's attention.

When I was casting a police drama, a wonderful stage actor came in to read for the part of an FBI agent. He had never read for TV or film before and had never taken a class related to it. He walked into the audition, wearing a pair of black jeans, which would have been OK, but he also wore a red silk shirt with wide flowing arms that looked like one of those Flamenco shirts. He clearly did not look like an FBI agent.

You have to remember that when you first walk into a casting, you are going to be assessed by what you look like physically. Since the client has not had the chance to listen to you recite your dialogue, they have nothing else to go on other than how you look. I'm not saying that if you're reading for a police officer you should wear the badge, hat, whistle and billy club. I'm saying that you might want to look more conservative and clean cut. You want to give the feel of the character.

If you are auditioning for the part of a nurse, you don't want to come in with the little hat and the stethoscope and the nurse's uniform, but you might want to come in wearing a pair of white slacks, a white t-shirt and white sneakers. You might come in wearing scrubs. You want to give the illusion that you are a nurse.

When you go to a black tie affair, you dress in a gown or a tuxedo. You don't walk in with your jeans and t-shirt and have the host imagine what you would look like all dressed up, do you? Think of your audition as a particular affair. When you walk in, we want to feel like you belong at that party.

Many times you'll hear that you shouldn't wear all white or all black on an audition. What are you going to wear if you are auditioning for the part of a widow who is at the funeral of her slain police officer husband? Yes, all black. Or, let's say you are auditioning for the part of a bride who is getting married on the beach. Might you wear all white? All cream? A flowing skirt and a little blouse? Most probably.

You may also need to get more info on your character and the set of circumstances surrounding the scene. Remember the story of our high-powered female attorney? She started off wearing the appropriate attire for an attorney, but because the script said that she was on a yacht, having an affair with her biggest client, her whole wardrobe changed.

I was casting a movie in conjunction with a Los Angeles casting director. She told me she hated when actors came in all dressed up for the part and she usually never cast them. I had just read an actor as a security guard and he was wearing his security guard uniform. I had already recorded him and sent her the tape. He was such a good actor and she liked him so much that she cast him. I asked her what her thinking was when she told me that she didn't like actors wearing uniforms. Her thinking was that she felt if an actor dressed for the part, as in a costume, he did this to overcompensate for his inadequacies in the acting department. This actor I brought in clearly was not doing that, but many actors do, so be careful.

My thoughts are that you need to create the illusion that you are who you need to be. If you are auditioning as a white-trash, trailer-park girl, you would not walk in with your nails perfectly manicured, your clothes neatly pressed, hair clean, and makeup perfect. No!

I have a set of sides I use in my class that is the part of someone who has been dragged out of bed in the middle of the night. She has been brought into her office to look something up for her client. What might that person wear on that audition? Would she be all dressed up or possibly in sweats? Would her hair be done or might it be under a baseball cap? Does she have full hair and makeup done if she has been dragged out of bed in the middle of the night? I think not. You need to think this way as well. You want to grab the interest of the client as soon as you walk into the room. If you are visually what they are looking for, then it is worth their time to continue on and watch your audition.

An actress was auditioning for the part of a wife on her way to work as a nurse. She was supposed to represent a simple, plain, nice girl. This actress walked in with full makeup on, tight, tight jeans, high spiked heels, and a very low cut blouse. She was very well-endowed and very sexy looking. The producer and director never even listened to her audition, as I found out afterwards, because she did not give the impression that she could play it down. I asked her later why she hadn't gotten dressed for the part, as she knew what she was supposed to be auditioning for. Her answer to me was, "I was coming from somewhere else and I didn't have the clothes with me." Make sure you have the appropriate wardrobe with you. Remember, create the illusion. Once you get the part, hair, makeup and wardrobe on the set will fine-tune you.

Notes

Notes

19

They're Not Just Props

Whenever I bring up the subject of props, I always hear the same thing: The talent is told not to use props on an audition. I used to wonder why, but now I think I know the logic. I believe other instructors are fearful that the actors are going to use the prop incorrectly or that it will detract from the actual audition. I always tell the students I instruct that a prop is a wonderful thing if it is used correctly. Let me explain.

An actor came in to audition for the role of a very powerful businessman. He had no real action. It was just a conversation back and forth. He was trying to figure out a way to make his audition interesting. He was just supposed to be sitting in a chair behind his desk. He wanted to hold the attention of the director, so he decided to use a pen. He figured if he was holding a pen he could use it to gesture, make a point and just have something to do with his hands. He looked at an assortment of four pens: a plain Bic-type pen, a flashy, colorful pen, a gold-colored pen, and a Montblanc pen. He chose the Montblanc, because it exuded the most class. His powerful businessman would use an expensive pen, not some cheap thing he picked up on the run. This actor sat in a chair for his audition and began speaking. He held the pen between his thumb and index fingers on both hands, rolling it back and forth. When he wanted to make a point, he held the pen in one hand and pointed it toward the camera. This served to be a very useful and powerful tool.

Another wonderful prop is your basic dirt-brown clipboard. This prop can be used for so many characters. You can use it if you are a worker, such as a secretary, nurse, doctor, government employee, office worker, bus driver, teacher and so many more. You can cheat with a clipboard also, by having your sides on it in case you need to glance at them. Many times, an actor doesn't know what to do with his arms or hands and this is a perfect prop to make your physicality look more natural.

I tell my classes that a simple prop can really enhance your audition. One day, an actor came in to audition as a security guard who was playing chess with another guard. He arrived with a small chess set that contained lots of little pieces. RULE #1: Keep the props simple! As he pulled the chess set out of the little plastic bag, pieces fell on the floor. He picked a piece up, only to have another one fall. He picked that one up and another piece took its place. The producer was very patient for many seconds, but then he finally asked—told—the actor to put this prop away and to just get on with the audition. The actor was determined to use this prop. No, no, no! If the producer or director asks or tells you not to use it, put it away! Please adhere to that. By the time this poor actor set up his chess set and began his audition, he was all flustered. The producer was already over him and wanted to get him out of there and to see the next audition. Everybody, including the actor, was distracted.

You know the term *KISS*, keep it sweet and simple? Apply that to props. When I suggest that you use a prop and keep it simple, that is exactly what I mean. If you are auditioning as a secretary who works in a lower class office and you want to convey that you are not the sharpest crayon in the box, what prop might you use? You could bring in an Emery board to file your nails or maybe some fashion magazine to leaf through. These are portable props that are easy to carry in and use on an audition. If you are going to use a prop, you must practice with that prop when you are rehearsing your dialogue *before* your actual audition. If you're going to use a prop, commit to it. Use it properly.

A prop is meant to enhance your audition, not detract from it. If you are going to use a pen, don't keep the cap on it while you're pretending to write. Make sure your pencil is actually sharpened. Don't just scribble with a pen—write something. If you have a watch on and you want to look at it to check the time, don't just pretend to glance at it and then look away. Actually raise your wrist to your eyes, look at the time, read it and then give your line. If you need reading glasses to look at that watch, then put them on to look at the time, and then take them off when you look up. Use the reading glasses as you actually would use them in your everyday life.

I was casting a feature film with an Oscar-winning director in my office. The director and I were the only two people in the casting room. The next actor came in and his dialogue was supposed to take place while talking on a telephone. Instead of bringing in a cell phone or a portable phone, he looked around my office quickly to see what he could use as a phone. He went over to a table and picked up a dry erase board eraser, and before I had a chance to tell him to put it down, he began his audition. You see, one side of this eraser was filthy dirty, with solid black ink embedded in it. Luckily, he didn't put that side against his face, but the ink was all over the palm of his hand. In the middle of the audition, he hung up the phone. He put this eraser down and continued talking. For some reason, he kept touching his face with the open palm of the hand that had been holding the eraser. Each time he touched his cheek, forehead, nose or chin, he would smear black ink all over that spot on his face. I was reading with him so I couldn't just stop in the middle of the audition. As he got deeper and deeper into his audition, his face got blacker and blacker with ink and I started to laugh harder and harder. I cannot even believe that I was able to finish that audition I was laughing so hard.

When the audition was over, this actor left and I looked at this big-time, Oscar-winning director and just about burst out laughing in his face! He thought it was pretty comical as well. We sat there and composed ourselves until we heard a little knock on the door. This same actor came back in to apologize. When he had walked out into the waiting room, all of the other actors wanted to know what was all over his face. He said he had no idea what had happened to his face. I had to stop laughing long enough to explain what he had done. This poor actor was mortified and he never came back to my office to audition again, because he was so embarrassed. This is a wonderful reason why you should not pick up a prop at the last minute when you are not familiar with it.

On another occasion when an actor needed to use a phone for his audition, he unhooked the receiver from my fax machine and walked into my casting room all ready. I looked at this familiar item in his hand and asked him to please put it back before he continued, since my fax machine would ring busy if this was removed.

Let's say your character is giving a business card to someone. Do you bring in one business card and strategically place it in one of your pockets, so that you can pull it out as soon as you need it? Or do you place many business cards in your wallet or purse and have to fish for it for a few seconds, as you would in real life? When I watch an audition, I want to see what reality looks like, not something contrived.

On one of my auditions, there was one line of dialogue that read, "Here's the file you requested, sir." It's not a very difficult sentence to learn in a matter of seconds. All of the actors who came in to read did the same thing. They looked right into the lens of the camera and recited the line. I would then say, "Where?" They would follow that by looking back down at their sides and telling me they had no more dialogue. I would ask them to do it again at this point. We'd go round and round until I asked them to show me the file. Can you imagine watching a TV show where a file clerk walks into the office of a police lieutenant, announces that he has a file, but gives him nothing? Where is the file I requested? Where? If you are auditioning, you can use your sides to hand over, or if you are a bit more creative, you can bring in a manila folder. Let's say you bring in several manila folders, and, as you are saying your line, you leaf though the folders, then present one file to the other person. You can take one line of dialogue and really make it come to life. You don't want to just stand there. If you are going to go to the trouble of having a prop at the audition, then go for it one hundred percent.

I was casting a cop show for the part of a drug dealer. This drug dealer was supposed to present a briefcase full of cocaine packages. I had three actors on the callback session. All three of them were fine actors and could have played the part. All three of them also brought in a briefcase. The first actor did his dialogue and when it was time to open this briefcase for us to see this cocaine, he opened a briefcase filled with papers, pens, a pair of glasses, paperclips, the usual stuff you see in a briefcase. For the next actor's audition, he opened a completely empty briefcase. As we watched this, we felt let down. The third actor performed his dialogue and when it was time to open the briefcase, we saw neatly wrapped packages of cocaine? Sugar? Flour? Sand? Whatever it was, it certainly looked like something we wanted in this scene. If all three of these guys went to the trouble of bringing a briefcase, why didn't they go the extra mile and prepare the neatly wrapped packages of the powdered stuff like the third guy did? Did this get him the part? I believe so. It just added one more element of reality.

Have you ever had an audition where you were supposed to be writing something? Maybe you're signing for a delivery, checking off a list, taking an order if you are a waiter, or taking shorthand if you are a secretary. Did you scrunch up your fingers and pretend to write? Did you actually go to the trouble of bringing in a pen and acting like you were writing with that pen but didn't take the top off? Isn't that crazy?

When you have simple actions on a casting that can be accomplished with a portable prop, then bring it in. Many times, the dialogue gives clues as to what props you may want to have on your audition. I was doing a casting where the actor was supposed to be wearing a tattered jacket. The other performer in the scene's dialogue told this actor that his jacket looked like it was falling apart. This actor had strategically sewn in random threads so that he could be plucking them out of his tattered jacket when the other person's dialogue indicated that it was appropriate.

This same actor came in another time and auditioned as a homicide detective at dawn. He was supposed to walk up to a crime scene, observe and analyze it. Before the audition, he stopped at a convenience store and picked up a cup of coffee with one of those peel-back plastic lids. Remember, you have to be memorized in order to pull this off. If you need to hold your sides, then you cannot attempt to fumble with a prop as well. What this actor did was to walk up to the crime scene, holding his cup of coffee. He recited his first line and as I read the other line to him, he peeled back the lid. He said his second line, and as I said my second line, he took a sip of coffee. Remember, the scene takes place at dawn, when all good cops are getting their shots of caffeine. What would complicate this audition is if that actor had added a donut into the mix. The cup of coffee was simple enough to pull off and not detract from his audition. The donut would have put him over the top. You have to practice with these props before you audition. You really need to be physically agile to be able to pull off swift and smooth movements. If you cannot do this in the comfort of your own home, do not attempt to do this in front of a director. If you add nerves to the mix at your audition, then you will end up like my chess-playing security guard and totally destroy any chance you may have of booking that job.

Props are meant to enhance your audition. They need to be small and not take away from your performance. If you are comfortable enough to use them on your audition, by all means do so. If you are not, then don't worry about it. As you get further and further along in your career, you will become more comfortable with the use of props at an audition. Avoid anything you have to set up. Props should be portable. Remember, less is more, and that's so true of props.

Notes

20
Slating in Character

What is slating? This is the way you introduce yourself on camera. There is some specific information that you must give on every casting, but the usual information is your name, the part you're reading for, sometimes your height, hair color, and profiles.

What are profiles? This would be a good thing for you to know before you are asked on camera. A profile is when the client wants to see what you look like from the side—your profile. You turn to the right and then you turn to the left. There is actually a whole art to profiles. Do you turn to the right and then the left like a robot? No. Do you slowly turn to the right, and then as you are turning to the left, you look at the camera, give it a little look and then continue on to your other profile? Perhaps. However you choose to do it, this is what your profiles are.

What is so important about slating? This is your introduction. This is the first thing the client sees when he is looking at your audition. If he doesn't like what he sees on the slate, there is no incentive for him to continue watching the rest of your audition.

I was casting a television series and looking for a character named O'Hara. O'Hara was a killer. With the name of O'Hara, one would think Irish. I knew this fabulous African-American actor, whom I thought would be perfect for this part, so I brought him in to audition. He was actually a really nice guy and not a hit man type at all, but I knew he could act the part. We rehearsed and when I turned on the camera, I asked him his name and for what part he was reading. He answered in a very friendly tone, "Hi, my name is Ray Forchion and I'll bet I'm the only black O'Hara you've ever seen." I immediately shut off the camera and asked him what he was doing. I explained to him that he had just told the director that he shouldn't get the part because black and O'Hara did not go together. I told the actor that I was going to start the audition over and he needed to be O'Hara from the time I turned the camera on until the time I turned the camera off. This time, he looked very serious while delivering his dialogue into the lens of the camera. He was very intense and someone with whom you definitely would not want to mess. Furthermore, he was now introducing himself as a really dangerous killer as opposed to a nice guy. He was booked directly from the tape and they didn't even change the name of the character. He owned that name when he slated on tape, and the director liked it. We have discussed this scenario in recent months and he told me how much that audition taught him. He has passed that information on to many actors whom he has instructed over the years, as well.

The slate has to represent who this actor is. Sometimes an actor will say to me that on the slate they want to do something completely different from their character, so the client sees they can really act. Believe me, directors want your slate to be as close as possible to the character for which you're auditioning. If they are looking for a nurse and three actresses come in and they are all of equal ability in their acting, and one of the ladies is a real nurse, more times than not, that is who will be hired. It is not that this actress will have to perform some medical procedure on the shoot, but the more authentic the director can get, the better. This is not to say that you should lie and profess that you can perform brain surgery, but you should make yourself as close to your character as possible and that starts with your slate.

If your character is supposed to have an accent, then you should slate with that accent. One of the things I always say is, "Never let them catch you acting." This is especially true when it comes to accents. An actor I was auditioning was supposed to be from the Deep South. He slated with a southern accent, went right into his dialogue with the southern accent and finished with the southern accent, never breaking character. The director loved him and booked him for the role on the spot. The day of the shoot, the actor went up to the director on the set and thanked him for hiring him. There was no accent. The director freaked out and asked the actor where his southern accent was. The actor told him not to worry, that he would have it for the shoot. If the actor had slated without that southern accent and then put it on for the dialogue delivery, that director would not have hired him as he was looking for real southern accents.

I was casting a part called Hit Man for a cop show. An actor came in whom I had never met before. He wore a suit, like a hit man would. The actor had a very cold personality. He came in, did his audition and left. I didn't like him, but then again, I wasn't supposed to like him. I was selecting the callbacks for this project. I thought, even though he rubbed me the wrong way, I should give him a callback, since he was a very good actor. That is the bottom line, after all. The day of the callback, the director saw me before the session. He excitedly told me he had found the perfect hit man. I was thrilled and asked him where. He told me he had found the perfect guy in the elevator. Well, unless this guy was still in the elevator, I wasn't about to find this perfect person the director had seen. You see, when a director finds somebody out in the field, as in a bar or an elevator, then his *find* becomes the standard to which every other actor is compared.

We proceeded with the callback session and in walked my cold-personality actor. The director hit my leg and told me that this was the guy from the elevator. I now know that unless this guy really messes up his callback, he will probably book the part. We finished the callbacks and the director booked the *elevator guy.*

I went back to my office and found our elevator guy, "Hit Man," waiting for me in the back of the room. I was not crazy about this guy, as he really hadn't been too nice to me all along. I wanted him out of my office. I told him he got the part, he should go home, and I would contact him the next day with all of the details. "I got the part?" he said in a childish voice. I slowly turned around and looked at this big, 6'3" hit man and wondered what was going on with him. He explained that his agent always told him to stay in character from the time he walks into a room until the time he walks out. "OK, "I said, "but what happened in the elevator?" I told him that the *guy* in the elevator is really the one who booked the part. He told me that he entered the elevator in his hit man suit, looking very menacing. Some guy approached the elevator when the doors were about to close. This actor stuck his arm out, stopped the door, and then stood up straight and tall with his back against the elevator wall. The director looked the actor up and down, and thought, Hey, this guy looks great. This guy would be perfect as my hit man. When the elevator doors opened, the actor went his way and the director went his way, now

142

taking with him a preconceived idea of what he wanted for the hit man role because of the actor he had seen in the elevator.

This scenario could have gone another way. What if that actor had been nervous in the elevator? What if he had worn shorts and a t-shirt to the audition, bringing his suit to change into when he got there? Let's say that the earlier scenario took place, but instead of putting his arm out to keep the doors open, the actor got nervous and couldn't figure out how to open the door. Instead of looking like a hit man, he'd look like a wimp and when he walked into the audition, the director would see the wimp from the elevator instead.

I have said over and over that you only have one chance to make a first impression. If the slate is the first time you are being seen by this director, then this is your first impression. If you want the part, the director has to see you as that character and that means from the beginning to the end. If you slate as one person, then transform into the other, the director may not watch beyond that slate.

Always start with your best foot forward. Speak your name clearly, as many people tend to mumble their names. Know the name of the character you are reading for. Know who your character is so that you can be that person from the time that camera turns on until the time that camera turns off. Don't break character during that audition at all. If you can keep all of these things in mind, you'll be way ahead of the game and much closer to getting the part.

Notes

21

Be in Character, Stay in Character

Never let them catch you acting. When you go on an audition, you want the producer and director to think that they are hiring the real thing. Many times, a director would love to find a real judge to play the part of one. Not that he or she is actually going to be officiating over a case. It's just nice to know, however, that if they had a technical question, they could ask this person. I'm not saying that you should go in and pretend that you are a plastic surgeon if you are not, but you should stay in character.

If you are auditioning for the part of a corporate attorney and you come to the casting in a nice suit, hair perfectly coiffed, nails manicured and you walk in chomping on gum, sitting with your legs wide open, this does not tell the client that you have the demeanor of this high-powered corporate attorney. Stay in character from the time you walk into the room until the time you walk out. This also includes waiting room time, bathroom time and the time you walk from the car to the office.

I was casting for an EMMY-award-winning television series. The casting had always been an integral part of this award-winning show.

The show normally shot in Los Angeles, but they came to Orlando, Florida, to do one episode. I was the casting director for that episode. One of the characters in this particular episode was supposed to be a fifteen-year-old, southern, backwoods, white trash, pregnant girl. She was supposed to be delivering a baby in her run-down trailer. The magnitude of the acting needed to be nothing less than brilliant. Usually a fifteen-year-old girl doesn't have the experience needed for a part of this depth. I had recently taught a workshop in the Orlando area and I remembered a girl from that class. She was actually in her mid-twenties, but she was brilliant.

This character needed to be sweaty, greasy, sad, and scared as she delivered this baby out of wedlock against her father's wishes. My twenty-sixish-year-old actress came in to the audition totally in character. She had dressed quite down, with oversized pants and a big blousy shirt to give the impression that she was pregnant. The audition required that she go through the motions of delivering the baby. She was completely focused, memorized, and did a brilliant acting job.

When she finished, the director asked her age. Technically, this question is not allowed on a SAG audition. The director could have gotten into trouble, but he needed or he *wanted* to know. I was standing behind the couch where the director was seated, but I was facing the actress. When asked her age, I knew that if she told him the truth, no matter how good she was, he would never cast her. I bit my lip and waited for her response. Without skipping a beat, she told him, with her southern accent, "I'm fifteen, sir." She never changed her facial expression. Her body language stayed the same and she never got out of character. As she walked out of the auditioning room, the director told me to grab her. He wanted to book her right then and there. I believe that if she had told him her real age, no matter how young she looked, the director never would have cast her.

The same applies for accents. If your character has to have a particular accent, then you must maintain that accent throughout the entire audition. This includes slating as I have said, and any conversations you may have before and after your audition. I was casting a feature film and the director wanted southerners. He didn't want actors to come in from New York and pretend they were southern. He wanted real southerners. I brought a gentleman in who is a very fine actor and he does a wonderful southern accent. The director started talking to him. He was interested in knowing where this man grew up. He wanted to know what types of activities he participated in as he was growing up in the south. This actor told him how he had grown up just a few miles from there and that he was a bass fisherman. He also told him how he used to go into the swamp and catch baby alligators. He did this all in character. He then auditioned for his part, in character, and when he finished, the director said, "Let's book him."

Many times an actor tells me that they want the director to see how they can act. They think that if they come in doing one character, as themselves, and then transform into another character, the part they are auditioning for, then they will be considered a really good actor. No! This is not so. Don't start fooling around with different characters. You need to stay in the character for which you are auditioning, from the time you walk into the room until the time you leave and then some. Never let them catch you acting!

Notes

22

Be On Time

Why have I devoted an entire little morsel to the subject of being on time? Because I feel that it is really an important trait. Author Admiral Lord Nelson said, "I owe all my success in life to having been always a quarter of an hour before my time." William Shakespeare said, "Better three hours too soon than a minute too late." As I looked up these quotes, I was amazed by how many were from various dignitaries who attributed their successes to being early—not just on time, but early. I have always felt the same way in my casting office. Time is money. You've heard that before. Well, in our business, on a set, time can cost an awful lot of money. Actors have been fired because they were late.

I was conducting a read-through of a script for a major feature film. A read-through is just that. All of the actors sit around a table and they read their various parts through the entire script. One of my local actors was supposed to be there. It was a paid read-through, which meant it was a booking, a job. This actor told me that he had a casting in the early morning before this read-through. I explained to him that he could not be late. He assured me that he would not.

I told him that if his casting ran late, then he needed to leave. As you can imagine, he ran late. All of the actors were seated, ready to begin and this actor had not yet arrived. The producer was not happy, as the stars of the movie were waiting in their seats to start the day. The producer looked at the production assistants, told them to lock the doors, and then he told me to fire the actor and re-cast. When the read-through was over, the actor was waiting outside the double doors of the conference room where this was taking place. He looked at me and I told him he had been replaced and there was nothing I could do about it. He knew he had to be on time, but he figured he could get away with it. He was incorrect.

There was an actor in my market who was very talented. I had known him for many years and had read him for many projects during that time. He had booked several acting jobs through my office. He was usually very pleasant when he came into the office, and since he was such a good actor, I brought him in whenever I could. Something happened along the way, though, and his ego got a bit out of control. His agent asked me if I could start my casting early one morning, as he had to be elsewhere. I obliged because he was a good actor and I wanted to make sure I presented him to my client. I arrived early that morning and waited. No phone call. No arrival. My actual casting began and this actor showed up fifteen minutes after that. No apology. No excuse. Just an impatient request that I see him right away because he was in a hurry. I had clients in the room who were waiting to see him, so I was obliged to bring him in. I wasn't happy though.

The next time he was supposed to see me, his agent asked again if he could come early. I told her what had happened the previous time and she promised he would be early, as he had to be at a shoot. The same scenario played out as the previous time. I told the agent I would not do that again. This actor never offered an apology, sent a note or gave any sort of explanation. In between those two auditions, I had booked this same actor on a movie. He was supposed to be at a read-through one morning. My phone started ringing off the hook at 9:00 am. He wasn't there. We called his house, his wife and the agent. No one knew where he was. He finally showed up about forty-five minutes late. No apology. No excuse. That was the last time I auditioned him.

This tardy behavior not only looks bad for you, the actor, but it also reflects poorly on the casting director and the talent agent who is representing the actor. It really doesn't matter how talented you are if you are not professional. You should think of your audition times or call times as appointments. If you had a lunch date with a friend, would you just show up thirty to forty-five minutes late without calling? Would you expect them to still be there? Would you still be there? Promptness is common courtesy. Nowadays, life is very busy. We are all running around in a hundred different directions. It's not like the old days. If you have an audition or are supposed to be on a set, let's say at 8:00 in the morning, or 5:30 in the afternoon, then you know you are going to run into rush hour traffic. Don't show up late to my office and tell me that there was traffic. There is always traffic at 5:00 in the afternoon. This should not be a surprise to you. Let's say you are new to the area or you are going to a location that you have never been to before. Plan accordingly.

I know actors who will take the drive the day before their shoot or casting just to make sure they know exactly where they are going. This way they won't have to worry about getting lost when they are on their way. If you are going to a very important audition, the last thing you need to deal with is getting lost and running late. This will throw you off and could seriously impair your ability to effectively audition.

When I interview for a big casting job, I always plan to get to my interview about thirty minutes early. If there is traffic and I run five to ten minutes behind, I still arrive in plenty of time to relax for a few moments before I have to meet and greet. When you arrive at a casting, there may be several things that you will need to do. You will need to sign in, possibly fill out a size card, read over certain instructions for the casting and any number of other things. If your audition is at 1:00 pm, you do not want to walk into the casting room at 1:00 pm. This is the surest way to mess up your audition. You will always want a few minutes to breathe, fix your hair, go over your dialogue one last time and just focus before you walk into the casting room. Give yourself a break! Assist yourself the very best way you can. You want to give yourself every possible advantage. One way to insure this is to be on time for each and every appointment, audition, and booking.

Notes

Notes

23
Nerves, Get Out!

One of the biggest audition inhibitors is nerves. When I introduce myself to a new workshop group, I introduce myself by saying, "I am a casting director by profession, and a human being by birth." People laugh and think that is so funny, but there is a reason that I describe myself like that. So many actors come into my office with such fear and nervousness at meeting me and for no real reason. I say no *real* reason, because the reason they have concocted in their heads is crazy.

Nerves are healthy. If you aren't nervous to some extent on an audition, you would be dead. Did I say that before? Understand nerves are a part of it, but a healthy dose of nerves, not some of the stuff I have seen. I have seen actors come into my office, holding sides, and their hands are shaking so much that they cannot even read the pages. I have also seen actors where the perspiration under their arms actually soaks their shirt. In addition, they have beads of sweat pouring down their faces. I had one guy who got himself so worked up that he had to lie down right there in the casting room, after saying he was about to throw up. People! It is not that big of a deal.

My all-time favorite nerves story came from a young man who was auditioning for a TV pilot I was casting many years ago. The New York casting director had come down to handle these auditions with me. He was a really nice guy. We were the same age and had both dabbled in theater as kids and really enjoyed the casting process. This young actor, early twenties, came into my casting room and we introduced ourselves. The New York casting director and I were the only people there from the casting side. We were seated, with a chair placed in front of us for the actor. I asked the actor if he had any questions. He said no, so we began the audition. In no time, the poor actor fumbled and choked, then stopped himself and asked if he could have a moment. We willingly obliged.

The actor stood and walked to the upper right hand corner of my casting room where I have a large silk plant. When he turned his back to us, I wondered what he was about to do. Then he began. He thrust his hands and arms forward and shouted, "Nerves! Get out! Get out, nerves! Get out! Out! Out!" and so on. I had never seen anything like it in my career, and I later learned, neither had my New York casting friend. We struggled to contain our laughter while the actor vented his nerves on my silk plant. When he was done, he returned to his seat and told us he was ready. In actuality, he appeared no less nervous. His hands trembled and his voice quivered more. We let him fumble through his audition, he left, and I had one more story to add to my repertoire.

I called this young man's agent and asked her what this display was all about. I was told that he learned that in an acting workshop. His teacher had given her students exercises to perform in order to get the nerves out before an audition. I guess she presumed the actor would know not to do it in the casting room in front of the casting director. I am telling you that any exercises you perform to get the nerves out should be done outside of the casting office.

I have seen push-ups, jumping jacks, deep-breathing exercises, running in place, squats, vocal exercises—you name it—performed in the casting room before someone's audition to relieve their nerves. This is not the place to do these things. The time and place to do your relaxation techniques is before you walk into the casting room.

I always ask the actors what they are nervous about, specifically. You see, if you get yourself so worked up that you can't function, you're not going to give a good audition anyway. This means you are not going to get the part. Just relax! I know, that is easier said than done.

Many years ago, I knew someone who got crippling stomach cramps before an audition. She doubled over in pain to such an extent that she couldn't walk and she had to cancel auditions. Immediately after canceling, the pain disappeared. She knew that nerves caused the attacks, but she couldn't do anything about it.

Nowadays, people take magic little pills, Xanax, Prozac, whatever. I personally disagree with this. Medication takes you away from connecting with your character. What happened to coping skills? This young actress eventually took an EST seminar, later known as The Landmark Forum. That worked for her. While I am not telling you to run out and take the seminar, I can say that after attending the EST seminar, this girl never again experienced the crippling pains. That certainly beats a pill anytime. What I suggest is that you search out workshops and seminars on techniques to combat nerves. There are meditation exercises, relaxation techniques, yoga, breathing—the list goes on and on. Just because a class doesn't specifically deal with actors or acting doesn't mean you shouldn't take it. So many outside classes can serve as companion classes to your acting workshops, and I highly recommend that you look into those, as well. Once you have the tools to deal with nerves, you can apply them anywhere.

I also strongly suggest some form of exercise on a daily basis. Even if you do a nice brisk walk for thirty minutes, preferably in the early morning, before you start your day. Any time, however, during the day, will help get the stress out.

Nerves are normal. Please understand that. Nervousness that includes trembling hands, soaking wet shirts, dripping faces and throwing up, is not normal. If acting is something that you really want, then go for it. You can't make it the "be all end all" where you're going to make yourself a complete nervous wreck and ruin the audition over it.

Always remember to breathe. Sometimes nerves will affect your hearing. It sounds strange, but they can. When you are nervous, your breathing can become very shallow and when you aren't getting enough oxygen to the brain, you can begin to shut down. So, don't forget to breathe. I feel this statement is important enough that I actually devoted a morsel to this topic. Nice, deep, slow breaths until you calm yourself down, put a smile on your face, and enjoy your audition.

A young girl walked into my casting room and before I even turned the camera on, she told me how she needed this job to pay off her credit cards and to catch up on her bills. Don't spend the money before you have even walked into the casting room. Don't put that kind of stress and pressure on yourself, which, in turn, makes you more nervous. Come in. Have fun. Enjoy the moment and then go about your day. The audition process can be a bit nerve wracking. You have to look at it as part of the process. The people in the room want you to be good and are on your side.

This audition process is not meant to be some harrowing experience that tortures you for days beforehand, ruins the day of, as well as the following days. If that is what the audition process has become for you, then you need to re-think this thing you want so desperately. If you still want it so much, then you must start investigating outside classes that deal with techniques to help you relax under stressful situations. You can't look at the audition as a stressful situation. Look at it as fun. You get to play. You can act like someone new, different, exciting. Go in there, give it your best shot, and move on.

Notes

24
Don't Make Excuses

I find that when actors come in feeling insecure, they begin by making excuses for themselves. I don't understand why someone would come into my office looking for a job and then discourage me from hiring them. This is self-defeating, but it happens more often than I can tell you.

This is how it goes: the actor comes into my office and hands me her headshot and résumé. This is presuming that she remembered to bring it to the audition. Then she tells me she needs new headshots and explains that this one is old. Next, I'm told that the résumé needs updating, as she has done several more jobs. Then the actor auditions, and immediately after finishing, without waiting for me to turn the camera off, she either facially or verbally editorializes. By this I mean she makes a horrible, way out of character face to indicate how terrible she thinks her audition was. Or, she says it was horrible. Have you ever done this? Well, stop it! Maybe, just maybe, I liked it.

This business of ours is so subjective that it is possible to change the client's mind by systematically telling him why he shouldn't hire you.

I came up with an analogy which I think makes sense. Picture yourself as the office manager of a large company. You are looking to purchase a new copier, as your old one is on its last leg. The copier salesman comes in and shows you a brochure for a new and improved copier, but he tells you that this is actually last year's model. He can only describe all the new features on this year's model. Next, he tells you he has the copier in the truck outside, however, it is missing the on/off switch, but you can always use a paperclip to remedy that. He then tells you that you'll need toner and sometimes the paper jams, but you can just open the machine and take the paper out manually. Oh, and he wants you to pay full price for this beauty. Are you buying or are you running away? Exactly! Why, then, would I want to *buy* an actor who tells me that his headshot doesn't really look like him anymore, his résumé is outdated and the performance that he just gave me wasn't really that good?

You are coming into my office as a sales person. The product you are selling is yourself. If you can't sell your product, then I will not buy it.

I was doing a casting for a TV pilot and I was looking for several of the series regulars. I had sent the sides out many days in advance. An actor came in to audition and you could tell he was a good actor, but he really wasn't doing a good audition. He didn't really know the dialogue. When I asked him what the problem was, he started making excuses. "Well, this past weekend there was a function that I attended and then on Sunday, I had to watch my niece because my sister went out." Excuse after excuse after excuse! He had the dialogue all weekend and he never made the effort to work on it. More excuses!

I have had actors come in and tell me they had the flu, a toothache, or a death in the family. They changed cars, leaving their materials in the other car. You name it! I have heard so many excuses for why an actor delivers a sub-standard audition, my feeling is that if you are involved in a situation that you believe will keep you from giving a top-notch performance, cancel your audition. If you come in and give a lousy audition, what would be my incentive to have you come back on the next casting? If you think offering me excuses will enhance your audition, you are barking up the wrong tree. Do you think if an Oscar-winning actress wasn't feeling well on a particular day that she would not be able to act that day? If she was so sick that she couldn't perform, don't you think she would stay home? She wouldn't show up to the set and give a poor performance. The same thing should be true for you on your auditions.

A local actor, whom I'd had the pleasure of auditioning on many of my projects, came in to read for a role on a TV series I was casting. The part would be an episode guest star. He was great. Then the producer wanted him to read for an even bigger role. We handed him the new sides and told him to go work on them for a bit. We said to let us know when he was ready to come back to read, and meanwhile, we auditioned other actors. In about ten minutes, he informed us that he was ready, and he proceeded to give another great performance. We ultimately hired him for the bigger role. What I did not know was that he had gotten out of his sickbed to come to that audition. He had a terrible flu with a very high fever, a sore throat and a headache. He is a wonderful actor, so his illness didn't affect him. He never made excuses that he couldn't act because he was sick. He just did what he came to do and went home.

Either you can act or you can't act. Excuses are not going to make a difference. If your trauma is that bad and will affect your audition, then do not go.

Another wonderful excuse I received from an actor who had seriously messed up on an audition for a series regular was that the pages were faxed to him backwards. I won't repeat this story, I will only remind you how an actor was not paying attention to his sides and memorized twelve pages backwards. That excuse does not warrant a pass. That excuse does not work because you, as a performer, should know better.

Excuses are just that—excuses. They will not make you look any better. They will actually make you look worse. If you can't handle a few pages of dialogue on an audition because of a lame excuse, why would we think you could handle it on a set? I have actually had actors who've had the nerve to tell me that they are terrible on the audition, but once they get the part, they are wonderful. You will not get the part if you can't handle the audition! Why would we think you would be any better on the shoot? Oh, sure, I can just see the director now, saying, "Wow, he did such a horrible audition. I think I'll hire him. Once I get him on the set in front of all the crew, the other actors, producers and director, I'm sure he'll be great." I don't think so, do you?

Keep the excuses outside. Even if you feel like you need to make one, don't! We do not care about your excuses. We only want to see how great you are. Don't make excuses to hide your insecurities. Take a deep breath, go in there and do your best.

Notes

Notes

25
Don't Forget to Breathe

I have entitled this morsel *Don't Forget to Breathe*. When I say this in my lecture sessions, I usually get some laughs and some strange looks. The first time I heard someone say this was when I was about to go interview with Burt Reynolds for the casting position on his television series, *B.L. Stryker*. I was nervous for two reasons. One was, of course, because I wanted to get this job, but number two, I was going to meet *the* Burt Reynolds. Most times when I interview for a casting position, I meet some producer whom I have never heard of before. This time, I was meeting with the very famous actor Burt Reynolds at his house! I had to figure out how to get past that in order to actually speak about my casting qualifications.

I went to talk to a friend of mine who happens to be a psychologist. I sat in my friend's office and begged him to give me some words of wisdom. I just had to get through this interview, which I had built up to monumental proportion. He looked me right in the eyes and said, "Don't forget to breathe." At this point, I was rather annoyed with him. What a ridiculous comment to make to me! After all, I was here looking for guidance, reassurance, sound advice and he was telling me not to forget to breathe? We started to discuss this rather obscure concept. He explained that when people get nervous, their breathing becomes shallow. They don't take in as much oxygen and they start to lose focus. Sometimes their hearing starts to fail as they become more nervous, because they aren't getting as much oxygen to their brain. I was listening a bit more intently now. I actually had experienced these things over the years. He told me that if I concentrate on my breathing that I will be calmer, more relaxed, more focused, and this will in turn help me tremendously with my interview. I left his office with nothing more than breathing techniques.

Breathing techniques are very helpful in many aspects of life. I remembered back to when I became a certified scuba diver. We had to learn how to breathe with this self-contained, underwater breathing apparatus, SCUBA. It was crucial that we breathe in and breathe out. I learned how to do it so well that I could make a tank of air last a lot longer than most. I knew how to take deep inhalations that filled my lungs. Once my brain and lungs were filled with air, I felt a sense of great clarity underwater. Maybe my psychologist friend was actually onto something. Breathing techniques are important in yoga, meditation and so many other relaxation exercises that I began to practice my breathing exercises before I went in to meet Mr. Burt Reynolds.

When you have dialogue to deliver on a casting, correct breathing can be very beneficial. Many times, an actor rushes through his dialogue on a casting, thus completely destroying any chance he had of booking the job. Proper breathing techniques help pace you, regulate you, keep you calm and focused. If you have not taken any breathing classes, find one. Get involved in a yoga or meditation class and start working on your breathing techniques.

When the day for our meeting came, I arrived early at the Reynolds' home in Tequesta, Florida. As I sat in the outer office, waiting to see him, I felt my heart pounding out of my chest. A light bulb went off over my head, reminding me to breathe. Oh, yeah, right. I had forgotten. The door opened and out walked Burt Reynolds. I followed him into his office, took a seat, and looked around the room, which was covered with Florida State University paraphernalia. I had started my college career as a University of Florida Gator and had graduated as a University of Miami Hurricane, so I decided to lay all my cards on the table. I locked eyes with him and said, "Look, I started out as a Gator and I graduated as a 'Cane, so if you want me to leave right now, say the word." He laughed and I just kept breathing. I don't remember much else about that hot summer afternoon's interview in Tequesta, Florida, but I know that I was calm, because I kept breathing in and out, in and out. Oh, and I did get the job. You will, too, if you just remember to breathe.

Notes

26

Be In the Moment

Many times when I conduct a casting, an actor will *physically* come in but *he's* anywhere except where he should be, which is in my casting studio. What I mean is that his focus is everywhere but on the actual casting. An actor came into one of my sessions and started the conversation by telling me how sick he was. This is not a good way to start a conversation with a casting director. The next thing he told me was that he couldn't wait until the casting was over so that he could go home and get back into bed. He had been thinking about this the whole time he was driving to my office, while waiting to go into the casting, and then he told me about it the moment he saw me.

One day I was casting a very big paying job for the actors. One girl in particular came to the casting and told me all the bills she would pay off if she got this job. She was so preoccupied with the money she might earn if she booked that she wasn't paying attention to her actual audition. Needless to say, she didn't get the job.

I once interviewed for a big casting job that was scheduled to shoot about two hours north of Miami and two hours south of Orlando. Before I even got to the interview, I began to worry that the actors wouldn't drive the two hours to get to the castings. Then I worried about where I would live, how I could afford another apartment in addition to the one I owned in Miami, where I would set up a casting office, and so on. I was so far out of the moment. I needed to remind myself that I didn't even have the job yet, so stop worrying about those obstacles. All I had to be concerned with was doing my best interview for this casting position. If I didn't get the job, all of those other concerns would never be a problem.

I had to stay in the moment, not get ahead of myself. I knew that if I got the casting job, everything else would fall into place. If I focused on the other situations, I would lose focus on the actual interview. Actors need to understand this concept, as well. Be in the moment. If you're not, you can completely ruin an audition, as you are not focused on it, your thoughts are everywhere but on the audition.

An actor came into my office and began our conversation by telling me that he needed to pay his child's school bill, that his car needed service, his credit card bill was overdue. Whoa! Stop! Was he in the moment? Absolutely not! If your mind is in other places when you audition, you cannot possibly audition effectively.

Many casting offices are in areas that require paid parking. Even though you should only be kept waiting one hour from your actual audition time, often you wait a lot longer. I've seen actors go into a panic right before their audition. Their mind is outside, worrying about the parking meter and whether they're going to have a ticket on their windshield. They are definitely not in the moment. If you go to a casting facility where you have to pay for parking, do yourself a favor, put extra change in the meter. Give yourself the necessary peace of mind so that you can stay in the moment of your audition and not lose focus.

Here's another obstacle that will keep your mind otherwise occupied. Do you have to go to the bathroom before your audition? Then go! Don't wait until after your audition. If you're focused on having to go to the bathroom, you're not in the audition moment. Trust me! This may seem like something small, but it's monumental when you are in the casting room and you really need to go. I know it sounds silly, but I have seen actors so focused on something that has absolutely nothing to do with their audition. I have gone out into the waiting room to call the next actor, only to have him or her proclaim that he was just about to go to the bathroom, but he'll wait until after the audition. No! I make them go before, because I know they won't be in the moment if they don't.

I do not want an actor in my casting room who is not there in mind, body and spirit. Trust me when I tell you that it is vitally important that you stay in the actual moment of the audition. If the casting director or the director gives you instructions and your mind is elsewhere, you'll miss some important part of that directive. Maybe the director told you not to do something and all you heard was the *something*, and you didn't hear the *don't*. Then you end up doing the audition incorrectly. The director doesn't realize that you haven't heard what he said. All he knows is that you can't follow directions and he cannot hire somebody who can't follow directions. Please, make sure when you go on an audition that you clear your mind of every outside interruption so that you're in the moment.

Notes

27

Have Fun on Your Audition

I know, you read the title of this morsel and said, "Easy for her to say!" It is easy for me to say and it's easy for you to do. An actor friend says that if he has several auditions in a week, it's a successful week. He tells me that his job is to audition. If he does his job well, he gets the prize, which, in his case, is the part.

Going to an audition is like playing. You're playing dress-up. You're acting like someone else. Sometimes, it's a bad guy. Sometimes, it's a wealthy business person. You could be a parent for the first time or maybe even a doctor or a lawyer. You can decide if you want this person to be nice, angry, high-strung or really calm. Yet, there are actors who come in so nervous and get themselves so worked up that they are visibly shaking while holding their sides. I've mentioned before, sometimes the perspiration under their arms is so heavy that it travels halfway down the sleeve of their shirt. I have seen beads of sweat just dripping down foreheads to such a degree that the poor actor has to incorporate wiping his brow with a tissue every few seconds. This auditioning process isn't meant to cause a heart attack! It's meant to be fun.

Think of the people who are auditioning you. They have chosen to be a casting director, producer, or director as their profession. They are neither better nor worse than you. They have just chosen a different avenue in this same crazy business of ours. Today, you are called *actor*, but that doesn't mean that tomorrow you won't be called *producer*. Does this make you any better or worse? Does this mean that you aren't as nice or as patient as you were before? I don't think so.

It's OK to come into the casting room holding your sides. If you need to glance at your sides to relieve some stress and to have a little more fun during your audition, go ahead. It's quite fine. Auditioning is not the finished product, but you want your presentation as perfect as you can make it to show the client what you are capable of doing.

Some actors who can't seem to have fun on their auditions make excuses for themselves. They say they're terrible at auditioning, but once they get the part, they'll be fine. That doesn't cut it. As I mentioned in another morsel, if you cannot do the audition, you will not get the part. So, relax.

You also have to be adaptable on the audition. Sometimes the director or casting director might ask you to read for a different part than what was originally given to you. Don't freak out. Don't get angry. Go with the flow. If they didn't like you in the first place, they wouldn't ask you to read for another part. Think about this, if you will: An actor comes in to read for a part. He does a lousy job, can't remember his lines, is a poor actor, but the casting director says, "Hey, I know, let's ask him to read for another part." No, I don't think so! If they ask you to read, that means they like you and there is interest.

When you go into an audition, look at it as a general read for anything. What I mean by this is you are reading for the person who is conducting the audition, not just for that specific part or that specific project. I have had actors come in who were not necessarily right for a role, but they do a great audition. I remember them as good actors and then bring them in again for something else for which they might be right. If you can go into the casting with a fun attitude and know that this is not meant to traumatize you, your audition will be a lot better.

Another insurance policy to make sure you have a good time on the audition is to be happy with the way you look. Have you ever gone out for the evening? Of course you have! When you like how you look, don't you have a better time? When your hair came out the way you intended, your shoes aren't killing your feet, the outfit you picked fits you just right, makes you look slim and trim and really enhances your look, and your makeup accentuates all your features, don't you feel like a million bucks? That is how you want to feel when you go into your audition. If you think you look good, you'll have more fun on your audition. You want to have all of your ducks in a row. The wardrobe is right. The sides are memorized. You have shown up early and relaxed. Your headshot and résumé are up to date. You have gone to the bathroom and fixed yourself up and signed in. You are ready for your audition!

You will be a lot more relaxed and therefore have a lot more fun than if you didn't have all those things in your favor. The audition is not meant to be a scary process. When I sit in the room with the producers and directors, please remember that we want you to be good. We want to give you every advantage. You see, if you are good, then we can cast you and we can move on. If you aren't good, we can't cast you and we have to continue to look for actors in those roles.

I've been involved with casting where a production had to be pushed to a later start date because we couldn't book an actor for a role. Time is money. If the actor cannot be found and the start date has to be moved later, this costs the production money. I want you to look good, because the better you look, the better I look. I like looking good. I've said that before. I can be the greatest, most fun-loving casting director out there, but if the actors I bring in are not prepared, if they are scared, messed up and don't do a good audition, then I have fallen short as a casting director. My livelihood depends on you. If you make me look good, I will continue to bring you in on my auditions. I'm not trying to put pressure on you when I say that. I want you to be perfect. Perfection does sound a bit scary, but someone will come in and have the audition down to a science and he or she is the one who will book that part.

You have to audition if you want a job, so have fun with it. It's not a life or death thing. Enjoy the process, even if you don't get the part, so you will at least have had a good time. Once you learn to do this, you'll start to relax more and parts will come your way. I guarantee it.

Notes

Notes

28
Perfume and Other Smells That Irritate

Nowadays, many people are very sensitive to smells—environmental, personal, cigarettes, you name it. There are doctors who treat people for diseases related to smells. Why am I bringing this up in an auditioning book? I'll tell you the story of a young woman who came to audition for me, as she had many times, but on this occasion, she wore a heavily-scented perfume. She was a lovely news reporter, who auditioned for acting roles on the side and who had booked many projects in my office. This instance was a callback session with a producer and the director for a movie of the week, and I was conducting the session as I usually do—I read with the actors and I also run the camera. I had just gotten over a bout of bronchitis, so my lungs were more sensitive than usual. When I opened the door between the casting room and the waiting room to call the next actor, my lungs filled with her perfume, which was so strong that other actors in the waiting room were commenting.

I began to cough. I brought the next actor in and coughed through his entire audition. The irritated look on his face told me that he was not too happy. I left the room after that and drank some water, in the hope that it would stop the coughing. It didn't. I asked one of my assistants to continue the session, and for the next two hours, I stayed out of the building, trying to stop coughing. Needless to say, this actress never came into my office again. This was not my doing. It was hers. She was too embarrassed.

On another occasion, I was casting an ongoing television series. An actor came in to audition, smelling like he'd just stepped out of a cologne bath. The scent was so strong that it lingered for hours in my casting room. All of the employees in my office commented on how overwhelming it was. I decided that I didn't want that actor in my office again. I would get headaches and sore throats, and it wasn't worth it just to be a nice girl and bring in this actor.

Every time his name came up after that, I told his agent there really wasn't anything for him. One day, the agent called my office and asked, "Isn't there anything that he could read for?" There actually happened to be a role that I thought he'd be right for, but I just couldn't deal with that stink in my office for another day. I could have just said, "Don't wear the cologne," but that's kind of hard to do without offending someone. I thought about it and decided that's exactly what I was going to do. I told the agent to tell him not to wear any cologne into my office. He was very grateful that I did that. He came in, auditioned and booked the part.

There are other reasons not to wear colognes, or perfumes or scented body lotions, creams, hair sprays and the like. Have you ever heard of *sense memory*, where a smell triggers in you an emotional response to something that happened in the past? Maybe the scent reminds you of someone, like the ex-boyfriend who dumped you and who wore the same cologne. You don't want to be reminded of him. Or maybe a mean high school teacher wore that perfume and memories of her are not pretty. The less you give the client to judge you on, other than your performance, the better.

Other smells can alienate clients, as well. Take alcohol and cigarette smells, for instance. I knew a wonderful actor who auditioned for me on many occasions. He invariably showed up for his auditions late, forcing me to make special arrangements for him, since he was such a good actor. Then he started showing up later and later and I noticed the smell of alcohol on his breath. This disturbed me, since I had, by then, booked him on a project for which he showed up late. This reflected poorly on me, and as a casting director, I have to keep this in mind. As I have said before, you are a reflection on me. If you come into the office, smelling of alcohol, I cannot, in good conscience, introduce you to my client.

Hygiene is another important issue. Actors have actually come into my office with highly offensive body odor. Are you reading this thinking, Is she serious? Yes I am, and it is rather disgusting. You see, the rooms where we conduct castings are usually soundproofed and often windowless, dependent on air conditioning vents to re-circulate the air. When offensive smells are all that's available for re-circulation, that makes for a very unpleasant day.

Have you ever walked into a fast food place or a convenience store where there are lots of fried food smells, or have you smelled them on someone else? It isn't too pleasant. Now picture yourself in the waiting room of a casting office where someone decides to spray her hair with hair spray before her audition. Those chemical fumes, not to mention the smell, linger in that waiting room long after that performer leaves. All I'm saying here is to be respectful, be aware of the smells that you might carry with you. They can affect your audition without your ever knowing it.

Before you even open your mouth, there is something else that can affect your audition. You can alienate the client with something that you're wearing. What I mean by that is a religious or political symbol, unless your character calls for it. If you are auditioning for the part of a priest or a nun, by all means wear that cross. If you are auditioning as an activist, by all means, wear that anti-abortion t-shirt, but if it serves no purpose in the audition, stay away from anything controversial. There is no place in a casting office for religious symbols or political views. You do not want the director or client to judge you on anything other than your performance, so make sure you don't give them any ammunition. This goes for ANYTHING controversial. You want to make sure that you, the actor, are the only thing being judged, not your religious convictions, political beliefs or particular smells.

Notes

Notes

29
Sabotaging Yourself

The art of sabotage is alive and well in the auditioning room. When an actor goes to an audition, the process is challenging enough without the added stress of self-sabotage. An actor can do this in so many ways. I have seen this over the years and it just amazes me how wonderfully creative actors are when it comes to using words and thoughts to derail themselves.

Let's start at the beginning. The first sabotage is showing up late for the audition. This escalates to not knowing the dialogue, arriving without headshots and résumés, and a very popular one is comparing oneself unfavorably to other actors in the waiting room.

The following are just a few examples of things I have seen over the years:

I was casting a big studio film with an Oscar-winning director. I mentioned this movie earlier in reference to another situation, the one with the director who wanted everybody to have a southern accent. He told me he wanted authentic southerners, not actors coming in from New York, pretending to be southern. I was very specific in my instructions to the agents and the auditioning actors—make sure to have a southern accent from the time they walk into the casting room until the time they walk out. Since I was doing location casting in North Florida, all of the actors I was seeing came from that general area. I knew they had not flown in from up north. As the callback with the director started, he asked every actor about the area in which they lived and then he watched and listened to them perform their dialogue. I had explained to all of the agents and actors that this is what was going to happen.

Several auditions into our session, when the director asked an actor where he was from, the actor said, "Boston." Boston? I am silently flipping out behind the camera. "But you're from this area now, right?" the director said. "No," said the actor, who then proceeded to talk about Boston this and Boston that, now using his Boston accent. The director finally thanked and released him. The director was upset with me for bringing in this person from Boston. Never mind that this guy actually lived in Central Florida and had been residing there for several years. I called the agent to find out why this guy did that. When she asked him, he said that he wasn't comfortable lying.

It's called ACTING! Do you think that this actor got that part? No! Do you think I would ever bring him in to read again? No! He purposefully sabotaged his audition. He went on a casting, drove all the way to the callback, and then threw it away.

Another time, I was looking for the host of a travel show. This girl would be traveling all over the world with the show. It was a very nice, long-term gig. A lovely girl came in, and the director began their conversation with the usual polite question: "How are you?"

The young woman launched into a story about how she hadn't gotten enough sleep the night before, because she and her boyfriend had been fighting all night! She went on to say how tired she was and how glad she felt to have this audition, so that she could get out of the house. When she left, the director turned to me and said, "That's just what I need, a travel host showing up with puffy, crying eyes, no sleep and unable to concentrate on her dialogue."

If you are going to the trouble of getting ready for your audition, learning your dialogue, getting dressed for the part, and driving to the casting facility, then don't turn around and basically tell the director why he shouldn't hire you.

For a recent casting, an older gentleman arrived at my office. He looked at the sign-in sheet to see who else had auditioned for his same role. He saw the name of a very well-known actor, one whom he thought to be much better than he. Do you know what he said to me? "Well, if I was the client, I'd hire him. I wouldn't hire me." I said, "Don't say that." But he was insistent. "Oh, no, he's a much better actor than I am. He's better known than I am. Absolutely, I wouldn't hire me. I'd hire him." Do you know what happened after that? This actor came in and did his audition with me. Now, what frame of mind was he in for his audition? You don't want to do that to yourself.

I believe you should dress according to the part for which you are auditioning. As I've said, don't wear a business suit if you're supposed to be a white-trash, trailer park type.

When I was casting a rave scene for a new television show, a young man came in, looking very much like the character for which he was reading. He wore two earrings, a nose ring, torn jeans, t-shirt, disheveled hair, and had a couple of tattoos. He looked like he belonged in a rave club. He was a very good actor and he did a good job on his audition. I could tell the producer was interested. He asked the actor some personal questions, one regarding the design of his tattoo. The actor systematically took his entire *costume* apart for the producer, explaining that he was probably the straightest person the producer would ever meet. The tattoos weren't real. Neither were the earrings and the nose ring, as evidenced by the actor's extracting them, in front of the producer, from the pretend holes. His demeanor changed from brooding raver to really sweet, nice guy. The producer thanked him and cast someone else.

If you are going to the trouble of putting on tattoos, earrings, nose rings, and the like, then stay in character. It is unbelievable to me that somebody would go to all of that effort to put a character together and then disassemble it in front of the client.

Another popular way an actor can sabotage himself is by making excuses. Time and time again, this happens in front of me. An actor walks in and hands me his headshot and résumé. He explains that the picture is old and he's just waiting to get some money to afford new headshots. I don't need to know this. Then I flip over the photo to look at the résumé, and the actor tells me it needs to be updated. So, the actor has given me an outdated photo and an incomplete résumé. Wow! Thanks. Then I read the actor and when he finishes with the audition, he says, "What a terrible audition!" He makes a face that tells me what an awful read he thought he did. Well, maybe I liked it. Maybe I thought it was good. If you put that negative thought into my head, you might change my mind. I might think, Hmmm, maybe it wasn't that good after all.

Let me decide if your audition was good or not. By berating themselves, actors can kill an audition that I thought was good. He or she came into my casting room, handed me an old photo, an outdated résumé, called the audition *awful,* and then expected to be introduced to the director. Why?

As I've said before, you represent me. If you don't have confidence in yourself, why should I? Remember the copier salesman? Would you buy the copy machine from the salesman who tells you everything that's wrong with it? No! Who wants to buy damaged goods? It's the same with an actor. Confidence at your audition is a must. Don't sabotage your audition or your materials, because if you do, you sabotage yourself.

If you let them, other people can throw you off. One of my pet peeves is socializing in the waiting room before your audition. I was casting a series and there were two actors in the waiting room. One, the blond, was waiting while the brunette auditioned. I knew the brunette was threatened by the blond, because the blond booked everything he went on. When the brunette came out of the casting room, he quietly went over to the blond and told him he had overheard the director say they did not want a blond for the part. He then wished him good luck and left. The blond came to me with fire in his eyes, his face reddened. He wanted to know why I had wasted his time by bringing him in. Imagine, he listened to his competition, rather than trust the casting director. It was now his turn to walk into the casting room and you can well envision his frame of mind.

I cannot emphasize enough not to talk to other actors in the waiting room before your audition. Tell them you'll meet with them in the parking lot, coffee shop, anywhere away from the casting office, but *after* your audition. There is only one reason you show up to a casting director's office at a specific time on a specific day, and that is to audition. You are not there to catch up with old friends, make lunch plans or compare bookings. You are there to audition for a part and if your focus is on anything other than auditioning, you are sabotaging yourself.

Another thing you do not want to focus on is the other actors in the room. I have observed waiting room dynamics when several actors in the same category are there, waiting together. The better actors seem to walk outside in the hallway or find a corner in which to go over their dialogue. Some, however, watch their competition. When the competition walks in, they say out loud, "Oh, so-and-so is here. We all might as well leave, because he's going to book this." That may flatter that actor, but it changes the focus of the actor or actors who are speaking. If you focus on the other actor and that actor also focuses on himself, who is going to focus on you? All of the energy goes away from you.

Don't worry about the other actor. I guarantee he is thinking the same thing about you without showing it. Also, if I hear you make these comments, *I* pay more attention to the actor you are praising. My feeling is that if his competition is worried about this actor, he is probably good and I should take notice. Makes sense, doesn't it?

Many times I am told that the talent may not even be available on the shoot date. One of my producers had narrowed a role down to three actors. Prior to the audition, one of the three informed me that if the part were to shoot on one of the scheduled shoot dates, he would not be available. If the part shot on the other two days, he would be fine. After the casting, the producer informed me that this part would indeed work on that one day the actor had told me he would not be available. I informed the producer not to even consider this person, because he had made it clear he couldn't be available on that day.

Several days after this callback session, that actor phoned and wanted to know why he didn't get the part. I explained that he had been their number one choice, but since the shoot date would be the one day he wasn't available, I told them not to consider him. This actor got very upset with me. Why? Because the truth of the matter was he had auditioned for something else scheduled to shoot that day. The actor had been so sure that he would get the other project that he decided to just tell me he wasn't available. It turned out he didn't get either job.

Let's discuss showing up late or right on time for your audition. *On time* means you arrive at the exact time you should be walking into the casting room for your audition. As I said in the *Be On Time* morsel, don't do this. Always aim to be in place thirty minutes early. Allow for everything: traffic, parking problems, weather. Once you're inside, you have time left to get yourself together before your audition. The last thing you need is to pull into the parking lot on time, only to discover you can't find a spot for your car, you need change for the meter, or you have to park blocks away. This will put you into a panic. The heart rate goes up. Your focus shifts to getting to the audition on time instead of the audition itself. When you finally do find that parking space, you then have to run to the casting. Once you enter the waiting room, you're still not ready. You have to get your headshot and résumé ready, sign in, look at yourself one last time, make sure your clothes are on straight, and possibly, look at your dialogue one more time. It's your turn and you don't want to keep them waiting. You will be completely thrown off by all of this. Trust me, it will sabotage you.

You have a lot to deal with when you go to a casting. So many variables are not in your control at an audition, make sure you don't sabotage the ones you can control.

Notes

30
The Waiting Room

The waiting room is an interesting space. The dynamics in this space are something special. This is where nerves can do a number on your head. This is where you start to doubt yourself, where you look over your competition and imagine all sorts of things. This is where you check out the people sitting near you and wonder why they're wearing what they are. Be very careful in the waiting room or this is the place that causes you to mess up your audition.

On one occasion, I observed the women in my waiting room—some were seasoned actresses and a few were novices. One of the more experienced actresses walked over to a very pretty, young actress who was sitting nice and tall in her chair. In a very demeaning tone, the experienced actress asked the younger woman why she had chosen what she was wearing. In a matter of seconds, I watched this girl go from a confident-looking young lady to a sad-faced person, slumped in her seat.

Another time, I was conducting a television show audition. Several times I announced that no one should leave the waiting room after their audition. This was to be a very quick turn-around, where the director would pick the actress right away, whisk her off to wardrobe, and get her ready to shoot the next day. One by one, the actresses came in to meet the director. After he had seen all of the actresses once, he wanted to see them all again. I looked for one actress in particular. She wasn't there. We checked down the hall, in the bathroom, everywhere. When I asked the room if anyone knew where she was, two actresses smiled and told me she had left. I asked if they had heard my announcement and indeed they had. I tried to call on her cell phone, but there was no signal at the hotel where we were casting, so I couldn't find this poor actress. She was the director's favorite, but since he couldn't see her again, he ended up going with another girl. He did not go with either of the two girls whom I had asked about the favorite's whereabouts. The next day, I reached the director's favorite on the phone, who was quite upset at hearing of her loss. She told me that when her audition was over, she asked her two *friends* if she should stay or go. They advised her to go, so she did. Those two actresses were her competition, but she thought they were friends. They heard me make the announcement, yet they told her to go. Please remember, the people you are auditioning against are your competitors. I always say that if they're going to pay your mortgage, your bills, or your child's tuition, then, by all means, listen to them. If not, listen to the casting director or whoever is in charge.

Another thing you don't want to do is ask another actor to run lines if he's auditioning for the same role as you. I've seen two actors in the waiting room, reading their dialogue with one another, and one of the actors continuously messes up the lines when reading with the other actor. This is done in a very subtle way, but it can be rather costly and many times it's a very intentional mistake.

The waiting room is the place you stay right before your audition. The energy in there is very tense, at best. People have a tendency to converse to try to relax, but they should be running their lines instead. I saw a very focused actor running his lines before an audition. Another actor came out of his audition for the same character. He approached the first actor and tried to strike up a conversation. The actor who was preparing for his audition tried to walk away from the actor who was finished. The first actor continued to pace and rehearse, while the second actor followed him, trying to chat. Finally, the first actor told the second actor that he had to work on his lines and he walked away.

This actor had a very large booking ratio and one of his preparation techniques was to stay focused and work on his dialogue before an audition. He went in, did his audition and then left. He and I spoke afterwards and he told me how upset he was to have dismissed that actor. I asked him if that actor had his phone number. "Yes," he said. I asked if that actor had his email address. Again, his answer was a yes. I asked if that actor ever called or emailed him. When he told me that he never had, then I told him he had nothing to be upset over and he owed the other actor nothing.

When you enter the waiting room, make sure you fill out all paperwork necessary and sign in. Make sure you sign in on every sheet that is put out and make sure your handwriting is legible. I have two sign-in sheets when I conduct a casting. One is the SAG sign-in sheet and the other one is a phone number/email sheet. It is amazing how many actors don't sign in on this sheet, or if they do, they don't fill it out correctly. If we ask for your phone number, make sure we can read it and make sure we have your area code. If we ask for your agent, don't just write "Debbie." We don't always know who Debbie is, and we don't always know who all of the assistants are at an office, but we do know the name of the agency.

Another important factor that you have to keep in mind is sometimes your casting might be quick, while somebody else might be in the casting room for five or more minutes. Please, don't think if somebody is in the casting room longer than you their chances of getting the part are better than yours. Theirs are not better. Sometimes an actor might come into my casting room and they might be an old friend of mine whom I haven't seen in a while. I conduct their audition and afterwards we may chat for a few minutes. If you come in and I don't know you, your time in the casting room may be much quicker. Maybe you do an excellent job and I don't have to work with you. You're in and out. Please, understand that the amount of time an actor is in the actual casting room is not indicative of whether or not they're going to book the part.

When you arrive, you may want to go to the bathroom, to fix your hair and makeup, to review your dialogue, or any number of things. You want to show up early enough to get yourself situated and organized. Sometimes you get to an audition and you are informed in the waiting room that your part has been written out and you are going to be given new dialogue. This is not a fun position to be in, but if you are early and have some time to look over the dialogue, you should be OK.

There are people in the waiting room who are energy vampires. What I mean by energy vampire is that they suck the energy right out of you. Make sure if somebody comes over to you in the waiting room and you feel your energy being sucked away, politely excuse yourself. Go somewhere else, if you have to, even if that means walking out into the hallway. The waiting room is a necessary evil part of the audition. Make sure that you approach it from a positive standpoint. Understand that you are there for yourself and no one else. As long as you keep that in mind, you should do a very good job on your audition.

Notes

Notes

31
Horror Stories

What are horror stories and why am I mentioning them in this book? A horror story is something you tell in the audition that pushes a client away, that causes them not to want to hire you. In another morsel I talked about the girl who came to a casting and proceeded to tell the director how she had fought with her boyfriend the night before, that she had been awake, crying all night, and that she was glad to get out of the house. That is not something a client needs to hear.

I sometimes wonder what goes through an actor's mind when they come in for an audition. Even if you know these clients from another job or place, this is still an interview and you must treat it as such. If your goal is to waste your time that day, then, by all means, tell the client something to dissuade them from hiring you.

An actor came in one day and I asked him how he was doing— the simple, generic, "Hi, how are you?" He said that his mom had just died. That was sad, for sure. Then, he continued to tell me that she had been his best friend and that she had died so young from cancer. He told me how, as a single mom, she had raised his sister and him and how hard she had worked for them. He talked about the poetry book he had written and dedicated to her and about how therapy was helping him. A room full of actors was waiting to see me. I needed to put the man on tape and to move on to the next person, but, instead, I had to listen to him pouring out his heart about his mother and his feelings.

Stop! This was not the time, not the place, nor the person for this. If I had cut him off in the middle, I would have seemed like a cold, heartless witch, but in the middle of a casting session, I don't have time to play psychological counselor. Eventually, I eased him out of this conversation and back into his audition, which was the reason he was in my office. I can tell you, though, that having this conversation beforehand completely threw him off, and he wasn't ready to do the audition.

When you walk into a casting session, think before you speak. Clients do not want to hear depressing stories from an actor whom they are considering hiring. Think about it. When you work on a set, you could potentially be with this client for ten, twelve, fourteen, sixteen hours. Who in their right mind would want to spend that much time with some depressed, crazy person? I wouldn't. Would you?

You also may want to think about the project for which you are auditioning. I can't tell you how many times an actor disqualified himself from the job by putting down the project. Take the actor who auditioned for a drug-using, nightclubbing character in a television show. This young actor came in to read and gave a really good audition. He should have just left it at that, but instead, he chose to tell the producer how squeaky clean he was, that he would never be caught dead using drugs or being in a club like that. I'm not saying that the actor should do drugs or admit to it, but I am saying just keep your mouth shut. When you come to an audition, we basically want to know that you can act the part. Do you have the right look? Are you talented? Can you pull off the read that the director is looking for? We really don't care about your personal life. We don't want to hear the horror stories of things that you're going through. Those things shouldn't enter into the casting process. Keep it light. Stay in the character for which you are auditioning.

Remember to think before you speak. When we say, "Hi, how are you?" keep your answer short. Keep it simple. We're just being polite. We don't intend for you to pour your heart out at a casting. Please, save your drama for the therapist's couch.

Notes

32

Words Can Help or Harm

I decided to write a morsel about the words we use and how they affect our lives and especially our careers. I have a little story to tell you. When I was first breaking out on my own as a casting director, I was approached by the producer of the *Miami Vice* television series. He asked me to interview for the position of in-house casting director for all of the principal speaking roles that were to be cast out of Miami. Up until then, I had been working for the company that handled all of the casting for the series. Since I already knew the job inside-out and backwards, doing the very same job, except now working directly for *Miami Vice* as their in-house casting director, shouldn't present a problem, right?

I was nervous. This was a big job, with a much bigger commitment and a much larger salary. I would work in the same offices as all of the production people, as opposed to the independent casting office some ten miles away. I knew I could handle this position, but my friends and family alike doubted that I could handle it. My parents said I should just get one of those nice little jobs at a talent agency where I would be making my steady $300 per week and be happy with that.

My so-called friends told me this job would be too overwhelming and I could never fulfill it. After all, most of the casting people down in South Florida had tried casting *Miami Vice* and had found it to be an overpowering task that they couldn't maintain. One friend even called my being the in-house casting director *a pipe dream.*

I had to distance myself from the negative people and their pessimistic words. I had to fill myself with positive thoughts. I walked around everyday, saying out loud, "I am the casting director of *Miami Vice*. Hello, nice to meet you. I am the casting director in Miami for *Miami Vice*," and so on. I didn't let up. When I finally had my interview, I was asked, "Can you handle the casting for *Miami Vice?*" My answer was, "Absolutely, without a doubt."

I said it with such conviction that anyone would have hired me, and I got the job. I had to believe that I was right enough to sell myself to someone else. I had avoided the people who tried to fill me with negative thoughts. I suggest you do the same. If I had hemmed and hawed and told the producer I wasn't sure if I could handle the job, what would the chances be that he would have hired me? None. No chance. My words had to be positive or I would not have been able to sell myself.

How many of you have family members who say your idea of becoming an actor is ridiculous? "Get a real job," they say. "What are you going to fall back on? Go to college. Get a degree in something substantial, not acting, for goodness sake!"

While teaching one of my workshops, I read a passage to the class from one of my *Chicken Soup for the Soul* books. Those books are wonderfully inspirational and instill so much hope in people. This particular story was about following your dream, and midway through, a student in the front row started to sob. He was a thirty-four-year-old man who worked in banking and finance. When I asked why the tears, he said he'd always wanted to be an actor, but his parents told him he had to get a *real* career. He was miserable. He had allowed his parents' words to keep him in a job that made him unhappy and kept him from fulfilling his dream of becoming an actor. After that weekend, he told himself that he could be an actor. He now resides in Los Angeles and is living the dream.

A few years ago, while casting the movie *Wild Things*, there was a role of a high school principal. I brought in several actors, but one of them stood out. When he walked into the casting room, he informed me that he would get that part. He said it with such conviction and determination that I knew he totally believed it. I got nervous for him. After all, it was a bigger role and I had heard that one of the stars of the movie wanted a friend of his to play the part. I was only putting local actors on tape *just in case* the friend didn't work out. I knew that, but I didn't want to tell this local actor, standing in front of me. I didn't want to burst his bubble. After his audition, he checked in from time to time, asking about the status of that part. I kept telling him I didn't know anything yet. He'd tell me the part was his and he was just waiting for me to actually book him. I felt bad for him and didn't want to crush him.

Guess what? At the very last minute, the friend of the actor wasn't available and my local guy booked the part. He wasn't surprised. All along, he owned it and he verbalized that. He had no doubts. He said he had walked around every day, announcing out loud that he had booked that role.

One of my very good actors came in to audition for me periodically. One particular day, he stood on his mark and complained that he never booked anything in my office. When he said those words, he made them so. At the end of that casting session, I told him to go home and say out loud that he did book roles at Lori Wyman Casting.

He needed to change. He needed to shift the reality. From then on, every time he auditioned at my office, he actually booked.

Your words and thoughts can really make a difference in the outcome of your situation. This applies to anything in life, but in this book, I am specifically referring to the acting business. Your words can determine how you feel about the task at hand and how others perceive you. One of the questions I ask actors when we meet for the first time is are they good. I want to know what the actor thinks of himself. It's a simple question, requiring a simple answer. "Yes," is what I need to hear, and presumably, if you're in the casting office, you want to impress me. One day, after asking someone, "Are you a good actor?" he fidgeted in his chair, looked around and stuttered a bit before saying, "Yeah, I guess." Let me tell you something: *Yeah, I guess* will not sell me on your talent. I must hear a resounding *yes!*

If you don't believe in yourself, why should I? If you can't sound confident and self-assured that you are indeed an excellent actor, then I am not interested in you. Don't forget, I have to sell you to my client. My job depends on you. If you are not very good, or you don't sound very confident in an interview situation, then you are going to make me look bad. My client will wonder why I brought him a mediocre performer. The next time he needs to cast something in my town, he'll go to the next casting director. I definitely do not want that! If it means that you have to practice saying out loud that you are an excellent actor, you are the best, you are better than the rest, then practice away. That's part of the game of being an actor.

You must have confidence and it has to come out in your words and thoughts. I know you are constantly being rejected. This business is weird. In most jobs, you interview maybe twenty, fifty, eighty times before you get a job. Then you get a job and you work maybe six months, a year, two, or more. In your profession as an actor, you audition maybe twenty, fifty or eighty times and then you book. Yay! You work for a day or two or even many weeks and then you go through this process all over again. You'll experience more rejection than just about any other profession out there. It's part of the deal. You have to get used to that. It's hard, but you have to do it.

My suggestion is to change the words you use. Sound positive in your convictions. You've heard the line, "Never let them see you sweat." Well, that's right. Sound like you totally believe in yourself, even when you have a bit of doubt. Reassure yourself out loud. Say the positive words you need to hear, over and over, out loud. You can't depend on others to give them to you so you must do it for yourself. Change your words and you can change the outcome of so much.

Notes

33
Don't Take Things Personally

I have found that most actors take things personally. If I don't smile, the actor thinks I'm mad at him or her. I want you to know some of the things that can go on behind the scenes, things about which you won't be aware when you audition.

At one point in time, one of the casting directors in my town was going through a divorce. Another had just suffered a miscarriage and another's husband was going to jail for a drug offense. Can you imagine walking into one of those offices at that time? Do you think the casting director might not be all sweetness and smiles? Maybe they were just going through the motions.

Right after my mother passed away, I had several weeks of nonstop work. My head was spinning. I went through the motions, doing my best to keep a smile on my face, but sometimes it just wasn't there. If an actor walked into the office and asked how I was, maybe I didn't want to make small talk. I may have just wanted to get their audition over for that day. Keep in mind that the casting director is a human being, first and foremost.

I auditioned this one actress several times in the past, but our relationship was nothing more than business. Then one day she came to my office, and before her audition, she told me she thought I hated her. First, that put me on the defensive. Next, it made her feel very insecure in that room with me. I explained that hate was a very strong word, that I didn't know her well enough to hate her. At that point, she felt worse than when she walked into the room. She never came back to my office—her choice, not mine.

On another occasion, an actress friend called in hysterics. I thought someone had died. When I asked what the problem was, she said she'd been on a casting with another casting director, and during her audition, he looked at his watch. I've checked my watch at times during someone's audition, so I didn't think this was such a terrible thing. She interpreted it as his being bored with her audition, that he didn't like her, and he wasn't interested in her. She went on to say that he obviously thought she wasn't a good actress and she probably had no shot at getting the part.

Wow! I explained to her that I often look at my watch and it's nothing personal against the actor. Maybe I'm hungry and wonder when lunch is. Since I have to keep a strict schedule when casting a SAG project, I may look at my watch to make sure the actors have not been waiting too long. None of this has anything to do with the actor in front of my camera. If the camera is running and I don't have to deliver any dialogue, then I might just be watching them. Yes, this may be the tenth or twentieth time I've heard the same dialogue, so maybe I need to take a mental break. That's not a personal attack on that actor. You have to realize that it can get very tedious behind that camera, listening to the same dialogue all day, sometimes day after day, so we may need that mental break from time to time. There's nothing personal in the action.

Another incident where an actor took an audition personally happened when I was doing a TV series. We were looking for a TV reporter. Since a TV reporter can be either sex and any ethnicity, I brought in a range of people. We narrowed our selection down to a very blond male and an Hispanic female. Both of these people were quite good and could have easily played the part. The director of this particular episode was a woman and the producer was a man. She wanted the female reporter and he wanted the male reporter. They argued back and forth in my casting office. She told him that he got the last actor he wanted and she wanted this one. After many minutes of deliberation, she finally won. We would book the female reporter. The next day, the blond male actor called in quite a huff. He wanted to know what the problem was and why hadn't he booked the role. He knew he was perfect for it and had done such a great audition. I told him he was the wrong sex and then told him the story. Nothing personal—just the wrong sex that day.

I have found that many directors do not like to shake hands with the actors. I have become more and more that way, as well. If you extend your hand and the director doesn't take it, leave it at that. Don't try to force the issue. If the director has never met you before, you can't possibly take it personally.

One particular actress I knew was perfect for a role, and hands down, she should have booked it. But, upon entering the casting room, she extended her hand to the director, who responded by folding her arms across her chest. Since the director didn't know this actress, the action wasn't personal, but the actress's face turned bright red. She got all flustered and could not perform her lines. We gave her several chances, but each and every time, she could not get through the dialogue. She allowed herself to take this hand gesture personally. Please, realize, if you have never met a director, a casting director, or a producer before and they do something that seems rude to you, it cannot be personal. They don't know you.

Many years ago, I went to Los Angeles on a business trip. I had worked very hard to set up an appointment to see a particular head of casting at one of the biggest studios. Walking in, I felt a bit nervous, but I was determined to get this man's business. I wore a skirt, blouse, blazer, stockings and heels, and carried my little briefcase with my casting résumé, as well as a three-page, color fold-out brochure. When I entered his office, he told me to sit down opposite him on the other side of his desk. He proceeded to put his legs and feet up on his desk. I found this very rude. As we chatted, he chewed on his fingernails, one after the next. I felt mortified, as I wasn't raised to act this way, especially in a business meeting.

When he asked for my résumé, I handed him the casting brochure that I had painstakingly laid out and printed in three colors. I was so proud of this representation of my work. He looked at it with what seemed to be disgust and asked if I had a plain résumé. I gave him my plain résumé on a single sheet of gray linen paper. When I asked him to take one of the color brochures, as well, he tossed it back to me. I was crushed. We chatted for about fifteen to twenty minutes more and our meeting was over. I walked out, feeling devastated. I had worked for weeks to get this appointment and this guy totally dismissed me.

In my mind, I made up this whole story that he hadn't wanted to meet me, but because I had been so persistent, he felt obligated. I imagined his assistant making him meet with me, because I had badgered her for weeks. I decided that he was angry about this, and so, even though he agreed to the meeting, he wouldn't make the experience a pleasant one. He'd show me! I wanted to scream during our meeting, to ask him why he was doing this TO ME. I kept my cool, though, and thanked him politely as I left his office. When I met up with my traveling companion, I told her what had happened. We were both mortified.

My mental story was all wrong, of course. After that trip to Los Angeles, I received many calls from this man, his office, the casting directors under him and many other companies that he referred to me. As a matter of fact, over the years, I have received so much business, directly and indirectly, from this man, I could not have been more off-base. What I found to be rude and uncalled for was obviously typical behavior for him. While I had interpreted his actions as getting back at me for forcing our meeting, he was simply being his comfortable self. How could I possibly have taken this personally when he didn't even know me? But, I did. Thank goodness, I didn't tell him, as that actress had done to me, that I knew he hated me. Be careful interpreting the behavior of casting directors, producers, directors and clients. If they don't really know you, their actions cannot possibly be personal to you.

Notes

34

What to Do on the Set –
Set Etiquette

So, you have made it to the set. This is good, but there are things you need to know about set etiquette. The first thing is to be on time. This does not mean that you arrive at crew parking at the time you are supposed to be on set, known as your *call time*. This means that you check in with the second A.D. (Assistant Director) at your call time. Sometimes crew parking is a shuttle bus away, which means that you park your car, then wait for the arrival of the van that drives you to the set, which could be as much as fifteen minutes away. You do not want to show up at the parking lot at your call time, only to find out that you have another fifteen minutes to wait. This doesn't make a very good first impression.

Once you are on the set, you must check in with the person in charge of your character. In other words, if you are an extra, you probably check in with the extras casting person or the P.A. (Production Assistant) in charge of extras for that day. Do not arrive on the set and sit there waiting for someone to come to you.

One morning, a stand-in we had booked was supposed to be on the set very early. He was a responsible person, so I didn't doubt that he'd show up. A few minutes after his call time, I received a call from the set, asking where he was. It turned out that he had arrived early and the P.A. thought he was the actual actor, not his stand-in, because they looked so much alike! This stand-in was ushered to the trailer of the principal actor and told to sit down. The stand-in was a bit confused, but instead of asking why he was in the trailer, he sat back and enjoyed the atmosphere. He should have asked why, because he knew he didn't belong inside that trailer. But instead, he waited, while the set looked for him, and finally, reached him on his cell phone. An honest mistake—but he should have known better.

Once you arrive on the set, you will be told to go somewhere. If you are an extra, it might be to a *holding area*, where extras stay until needed. Sometimes that's a tent outside. Sometimes it's a hotel room. It could be any number of places, but extras are asked to congregate together until needed. Do not leave this area, as this is where they will come for you when you are needed on the set.

If you are a principal, you should have your own trailer or *honey wagon*, which is a small room attached to a trailer. It usually has a little couch, sink, bathroom and maybe a chair. If you are not the star, this room is rather small, but it's air conditioned or heated and is a place where the actor can get away from everyone else. This is where you must stay unless you let the P.A. or second A.D. in charge of you know where you are.

Once you sign in, you're usually allowed to get something to eat, go to the bathroom, get checked by wardrobe or by the hair and makeup people. There's also paperwork that must be filled out when you work on a set. Completing this paperwork is very important—it means that you can get paid for the work day. It doesn't make sense to work all day if you're not going to get paid. If you're an extra, you'll be given a pay voucher. Read everything. Make sure you put the correct address on the voucher and that it is legible.

On one of my sets, an actor filled out his paperwork, then called me several weeks later to say that he never got paid. He had not kept a copy of his paperwork, so we couldn't see what he filled out. We contacted the paymaster to inquire about his check. It turned out the actor had recently moved into a new house, and when he filled out his paperwork, he inverted the numbers in the address. His check went out and then came back to the paymaster. It is really important that you keep a copy of your paperwork to track things like this.

Another time, I cast a very big, non-union commercial for an advertising agency. When a non-union job is cast, there are no guarantees that the talent will get paid. They usually do, but there is no union that governs them like a SAG job. This commercial was shot with a lot of actors on the set. After a couple of months, none of the actors had gotten paid, nor had I for my casting services. When I called the production company, which was in charge of paying everyone, they didn't respond. Shortly thereafter, the company closed their doors and filed for bankruptcy. When we contacted the advertising agency about getting paid, they claimed to have given the money for the crew and the actors to the production company, but they took the money and ran.

At first it seemed we had no recourse, but one of the actors on the set had retained a copy of his contract—only one! It's unbelievable that just one actor had gotten a copy of his contract after he shot that day. The contract stated that the advertising agency was responsible for paying the talent, not the production company. I politely reminded the agency that if the talent didn't get paid, they couldn't run the commercials. It was unfortunate that the ad agency had paid the now-defunct production company $500,000.00 to pay the actors and crew, but according to the contract, if they didn't pay the actors, they couldn't use the footage that had been shot. This contract served as a release to use the actors' likenesses. Everyone eventually got paid, but if we hadn't been in possession of that one contract copy, they might not have.

When you're on a set, signing your contract, things can get very hurried. The P.A.s scramble around, trying to get everyone's contract signed, and they don't want to take time to give out copies. You must demand one. You need it for your records. If you don't have a copy, you have nothing to refer to if a problem arises with that job.

Also, read everything before signing it. You are an adult and your signature is an agreement. If you don't read before you sign, you may be waiving your rights to something that you don't intend. If the P.A.s rush you because it's late, explain that you need a couple of minutes to review the contract and that you are not going to sign until you have read everything. Make sure that your salary amount is correct, that your personal information—address, the spelling of your name, phone number, screen credit, etc.—and your agent's information is correct. If it isn't right and you sign it, then you can't go back and tell them that they made a mistake. They may have made a mistake, but if you sign it, you have, in essence, approved it.

There was an actor whose name was spelled incorrectly on his contract. He barely glanced at it before signing because he was being rushed. When the project aired on television, his name had been misspelled. On a union project, if your name is spelled incorrectly, you are entitled to financial compensation, but since he signed the contract, he had approved the incorrect spelling, and he had no options.

Another faux-pas to avoid on a set is sitting in someone else's chair. If you've been on a set, you've seen the directors' chairs with the name of the actor, producer or director written on the back. When you see one of those chairs with someone's name on it, do not sit in it! That is frowned upon. Even if this chair remains empty for quite a while, it is not yours to use.

I was shooting a movie and one of the co-stars had a chair with his name on it. While he was busy working, one of the day players saw the empty chair. He decided to sit in it, since no one else was. When the principal actor came back, he was really miffed. It wasn't a pretty picture. My advice is to stay away from the situation. There are lots of fold-up or portable chairs available in sporting goods stores or online. You should get one, put your name on it, and take it with you whenever you work on a set. If you need it, you have it. Some sets are lower budget and they don't even have chairs for the actors. It might be worth the investment to get one of these little canvas chairs that fold up into their own bag, so you won't have to stand all day, or heaven forbid, sit in someone else's chair.

Being available when you are needed on the set is crucial. You cannot take off in the middle of the day. When you break for lunch, stay on the set. Time is money, and if the set needs you but can't find you, that's money wasted. Make sure you are where you're supposed to be at all times.

If you have dialogue, you will be given sides when you show up in the morning. Make sure you get them and make darned sure you know them backwards and forwards, up and down, before you shoot. You do not want to be in front of everyone on the set not knowing your lines. That is not a good place to be. If you need to barricade yourself in your trailer or to sit in a corner to learn your lines, then that's what you must do.

The more time you spend on a set, the more comfortable you'll become. Until everything becomes second nature, watch, listen, take notes. You want to be invited back, and the only way to get that invitation is to act professional when you are on the set in the first place.

Notes

Notes

35
Please and Thank You

Please and *thank you*, those little words are so important. We learned them when we were kids, and as we get older, they never lose their significance. We have a tendency to take these little expressions for granted, but we shouldn't. They certainly make a difference in helping your career. Remember how it feels to hold a door open for someone who just waltzes right through, without ever acknowledging your presence? How about in traffic, when you stop to let another car in, and they go on without even a hand wave or a nod? How does that make you feel? Those same feelings apply to our business, as well, when you don't acknowledge the people who do things for you.

If your agent sends you on a casting, thank them. If you book the job, thank your agent and the casting director who brought you in to read. How about thanking the director who actually picked you for the part? Saying *please* and *thank you* should not become a dying art. YOU CAN REVIVE IT!

If you feel uncomfortable with this sort of thing or you think it's really brown-nosing, well, it is, but in a nice way. People remember you if you brown-nose in a subtle way. I know it sounds a little like

I'm suggesting that you bring gifts. I am, but it doesn't have to be anything extravagant. It's nice to be acknowledged, so think about how you would feel in the same situation.

Assess an office situation where you want to give thanks. See how many people work there and how they look or act. For example, if the secretary is female and terribly overweight, you don't want to bring her a big box of candy. Maybe flowers or a pretty candle might be better. Gift certificates are always a wonderful expression of *please* and *thank you* and they don't have to be expensive. I think it's really important to acknowledge people.

I was casting a television series for which a particular actor really wanted to audition. He constantly sent me postcards, letters, little notes, invitations, and even random holiday cards here and there. He kept this up until I finally brought him in to read. I liked this guy, and he had endeared himself to me. Then, something very strange happened. He booked a part. I had actually swayed the producers in his favor, but I never heard from him again. No thank you note. No thank you call. No flowers, no trinkets, no candy, no nothing! This happened several years ago, and it still stings.

It's wonderful to be recognized for doing something nice for someone else. My job as a casting director is to bring actors into my studio, to audition them, and then to present them to my client. However, whom I bring in, is also my job. There are lots of actors out there, many as qualified as the next and there are casting directors who will not bring an actor in to read if they are a problem, unprofessional, or if, for one reason or another, they don't like them.

There was an actor in my market who was very talented. I had known him for years, and during that time, had read him for many projects. He booked a number of acting jobs through my office. He wasn't one to send notes or gifts, but he was usually pleasant in the office and he was a very good actor, so I brought him in whenever I could. Eventually, I believe that due to the large amount of work he booked, his ego got in the way. One day, his agent asked if I could start a morning casting early, because this actor had to be elsewhere and needed an early time. He was a good actor and I wanted to make sure I presented him to my client, so I obliged. I arrived at my office early that day and waited. My actual casting began, but this actor showed up a good twenty to thirty minutes after that. He never apologized. He never thanked me. He just waltzed right in.

Another time, while casting a feature film, we were having our casting session with the producer and director. By lunchtime, we were running a bit behind, and an actor who had a time scheduled after lunch showed up very early. I saw him in the waiting room and told him he would have to come back after lunch, because we didn't have time to see him before. He waited in the lobby. I continued bringing in other actors who had appointments before lunch, and this actor waited. When I finished auditioning the last actor before lunch, this guy pushed past me into the casting room, where he looked at my clients and told them he couldn't wait any longer, that he had to be seen right away. He did his dialogue, blurting it out once and then he left. I must say, I was so angry! Little did he, or anyone know at that point, but I was pregnant and needed my lunch break. Because we had been running behind, I was famished, tired, and needed to sit down and eat.

I later learned that this same actor had been on a casting in another casting office and was called in to meet the producers of another feature. When he walked in, the producer asked him to do the dialogue the same way he had done it before. The actor looked at him and said if he wanted it the same way as the original tape, he should, ". . . rewind it and look at the f-ing tape again." Then he threw down his script and walked out. Where, exactly, were this guy's manners?

We are a business of people. We are a service oriented business. Talent is very important, but a lot of talented people will never make it. Why? There is an art to this business, a game. You have to know how to play it or you aren't going to make it. Manners play a big part in making it. We are human beings first, and we like when we are treated as such. We have feelings, most of us, and we like them to be acknowledged. If you can apply the golden rule, "Do unto others," then you can see how it feels to be pushed aside or not even thanked when you do something kind for someone. I am not saying you need to send a Baccarat crystal parrot or a Waterford crystal letter opener to a casting director, as have been sent by actors. A simple *please* or *thank you* goes a very long way. A note, a card, an email, a balloon—something simple, just to let the agent, casting director or client know that you appreciate their time. Let them know you appreciate their faith in you, their giving you the opportunity to carry on with your passion.

Notes

Notes

36
Letter Writing

Sometimes, an actor will write a letter to the client for whom the casting director is working or to the Screen Actors Guild. These letters are usually not flattering. Rather, they are letters of complaint. If you have a legitimate grievance, then, by all means, write that letter, sign it, and be proud of it. If you don't, as in the following examples, then be careful what you write. It will come back to bite you.

Many years ago, I was doing a casting out of town. I had my lunch break coming up and I had scheduled a meeting with a client for that period. The last person in the waiting room was about to come in to be auditioned. I looked around the waiting room to make sure he was, indeed, my last person. Everyone else in the room had either been seen or was waiting for someone. One of those people waiting was my lunch meeting. I finished my last audition before lunch and shut everything down. This involved turning off the lights, camera, and recording equipment. Since I was renting out a studio, I was required to cover everything, as well.

When I walked back into the waiting room, purse in hand, an actor who was arriving late for his casting stopped me. I explained that I was taking a lunch break but he could come back in an hour, and when I began the afternoon session, I would see him first. He became belligerent, telling me he couldn't come back in an hour and demanding that I see him then. I reminded him that he was over twenty minutes late and said that I had to be prompt for my lunch appointment, so I'd be back in time to begin the afternoon portion of the casting. I was more than willing to see him first, but he had to come back in an hour. In anger, he took his headshot, on its thick stock paper, and threw it at me, hitting me in the chest. I was stunned. I actually began to shake and my heart rate went way up. This action was witnessed by my lunch client, who was standing there waiting for me. After this display, I told him, in no uncertain terms, not to come back in an hour, and for that matter, not to ever come back to see me again! I was mortified.

Weeks later, I received a call from the head of the Screen Actors Guild. He told me that he had received a letter from this actor about that day's events. The actor was somewhat accurate in saying that I shouted at him and then threw him out of my office. But he also claimed that I did so for no apparent reason. I asked the SAG rep if he thought that, unprovoked, I had picked this poor, unassuming actor out of my hectic day to throw out of my studio. I told the rep what really happened and asked for that letter to be faxed to me. As I read it, I was taken aback by the blatant lies this actor had made up. Sadder still was that this actor had worked with me previously and I really liked him. I thought he was talented and very marketable. Needless to say, I was never able to see him again. If you are going to write a letter, make sure it is accurate.

I was casting an ongoing television series in which one of the episodes involved three speaking parts for Japanese businessmen. In

South Florida, which is where I was casting, Japanese businessmen who can act and articulately speak English are quite rare. In this age of political correctness, I couldn't substitute Chinese, Korean, or any other Asian nationality for Japanese. I had to cast three men who perfectly fit the role. As we got closer to the shoot dates, our schedule changed. I informed these men of the new shoot dates. One of the actors was also a flight attendant and needed to rearrange his schedule each time ours changed. We scheduled him to begin work the following Monday.

On the Friday afternoon before the Monday shoot date, he phoned to inform me that he was going to decline the booking after all. He just couldn't take all of the date changes anymore. I wasn't too happy, but I couldn't convince him otherwise. Trying to find someone to replace him over that weekend was torturous for me, but we rectified the situation and shot the episode. A couple of weeks later, a SAG rep called and faxed me the letter that this actor had sent. He had documented everything that I had done: booking him, changing the date, changing the date again and again. He ended the letter by saying that, after all of that, I finally just fired him. He demanded payment for the booking and the subsequent alleged firing.

I said, "What?" I did not fire him! I had been sick over his quitting on me. He made my life that weekend a living hell because he quit. I needed him. I would never have fired him. Would you bring this actor in to read again?

There are casting directors out there who want to help you with your auditions. I am one of those people. My philosophy is that if you look good, I look good. I want to look good to my clients. I give as much advice as I think an actor needs. I have certain insights into a part that the actor may not. When I encounter an actor who isn't as talented as I want them to be, I give them ideas to bring the audition to a higher level. Such was the case in the next example.

While casting another television series, I brought an actor in to read for a part. I had read him before, but he had never booked. I liked this actor and really wanted to be able to find the right part for him. I brought him in to audition for a role for which he really wasn't right. He thought differently. I couldn't quite get the performance out of him that I knew was necessary for this role. I gave him certain suggestions and tried to help him along, but they didn't help. I had him in my casting room for twenty minutes, which is a long time to spend on someone who is not getting it. I really liked this actor, though, and wanted to help him. A couple of days later, I received a plant and a nice note from him, thanking me for working with him on the casting.

A few days after that, I received a phone call from the producer of this same series, who had become a friend of mine. He said he never wanted to see that particular actor again. I was shocked, as I liked the guy and had wanted to find a part for him. When I asked the producer why, he faxed a letter to me from the actor. The same man who had sent a *thank you* plant to me sent a letter to the producer that said I wouldn't know an actor if he came up and bit me. He continued that I didn't have a clue how to be a casting director and that he'd rather audition for anyone on the planet other than me!

Wow! I was certainly surprised. A couple of weeks after that, the executive producer handed over a stack of unopened mail that should have been sent to the casting department. As I opened it, I came across a manila envelope from this same actor, begging the executive producer to let him read for this same part again. Unbeknownst to him, that part had already been cast and shot. He wanted the executive producer to let him read directly for him, as I was incompetent and he didn't trust me. Of course, the executive producer never even saw that letter, because it had been passed, unopened, to me. When this actor got nowhere with his second letter, he wrote a third letter that he distributed to the SAG office, the local talent agencies and the local casting directors, excluding me.

The only thing these letters accomplished was to alienate him from me, my producers, many local agents and casting directors. He was labeled as *trouble*, and no one wants to deal with a troublemaker. So, next time you are even considering writing a letter, follow it through. Will it do more good or will it serve to alienate the very people you need to further your career?

Don't let anger or insecurities get in your way. Sometimes if you let a little bit of time pass, a situation will correct itself and all will be right with the world once again. If you think you're at fault about something and want to write an apology, think that through, as well. Sometimes, what you interpret as some horrific faux-pas on your part is really nothing to the casting director. Ask your agent to talk to the casting director to find out before you make a fool out of yourself by writing something. If it's warranted, an apology letter is nice, but it can hurt you if the party to whom you are writing doesn't even know a wrong has been committed. Take a deep breath, think, and move on. That is probably the best advice I can give you in this particular situation. If you must, write the letter, get it out on paper, and then burn it. This can be very cathartic for you, without burning bridges in the process. Think and then think again.

Notes

37

Don't Get a Big Head

Our business can make some very real people into monsters. It can create overnight sensations, if you will. We all know that there is no such thing as an overnight sensation. Usually the performer worked on his or her craft since childhood and no one had ever heard of them. All of a sudden, a big blockbuster comes out, and *voila!* An overnight sensation! Sharon Stone became one the morning after *Basic Instinct* came out. It happens.

In a matter of a season, our business also creates very wealthy people. How many times do we hear about the cast members of a TV show making a million dollars an episode? Remember *Friends? Seinfeld? Frasier?* Their salary doesn't include the endorsements those people get, as well as movie deals and magazine spreads. All that can be overwhelming.

This sort of thing happens on a local level, as well. I work in a market smaller than New York or Los Angeles, but the principle remains the same. People start off doing extra work, then move up to day players in movies or principals in national commercials. They make some real money. People notice them on the street, and all of a sudden, they are a bit of a star. The dream starts to come true.

I did the Florida casting for *Miami Vice*. Before *Vice* hit, Don Johnson had been acting for years. When the show became a mega-hit, Don was chased, yes, chased, by girls who wanted to touch him, to rip his shirt from his body. He had to hire a bodyguard. Think about that for a moment. You're walking down the street, or buying groceries in the supermarket, or trying to have a quiet dinner in a restaurant, minding your own business, when, all of the sudden, a group of teenage girls rushes up, screaming, grabbing for a piece of your clothing! That can be rather scary.

When those things happen to you, whether on a large scale like Don's fame or on a smaller, local scale, the attention can go to your head. It can make you think your stuff doesn't stink! I've got news for you, it still does. It's real important that you keep your wits about you. Don't blow all of that money at once now that you have more than you ever had.

I cast a series on which the entire crew was making tons of money. The star of the show made $500,000.00 per episode, and that was back in 1989. I made more money per week than I ever had, plus, I received a monthly living allowance that afforded me a wonderful condo right on the ocean. My office was within walking distance of the condo. Life, for that season, was bliss! But, I knew what goes up will come down. That's the law of gravity. I socked that money away like a squirrel stores nuts for the winter. One of my friends suggested that I buy a Mercedes, since I was making so much money. I didn't, of course. My Pontiac Grand Prix worked just fine. One crew member bought himself an $80,000.00 Ferrari. I looked at that car and shook my head in disbelief. People just don't get it. Our business is very transient. One minute, we're on top of the world, and the next, no one remembers our name. You have to strike while the iron is hot, or in this case, save while you are earning money.

You cannot let your ego get out of control, either. There was a time when I really wanted to cast a certain project, and I kept calling the producer, leaving messages, asking her to meet with me. I called no less than seventeen times. That might sound excessive, but I knew that I was a perfect fit for this project and I needed her to know me. When I finally had her on the phone, my other line rang. I asked her to hold for a moment. I put her on hold, answered the other call, then immediately put that caller on hold. Within eight seconds, I was back to her, but she had hung up. I was shocked. After all that calling and leaving messages, I decided to call her boss.

He called back after my first message. I explained what had been happening and said if this is how his employee conducts business, there was no wonder they were losing the biggest account they had. I don't think he appreciated my comments, but what I said happened to be true. Eventually, I heard the girl no longer worked for that company.

Fast forward three months and I was doing a casting. Guess what? The tables had turned. That girl was now an actress and her agent called her name in to my office. I was very interested in seeing her, since we had never connected when she was in her power position at the huge advertising agency. She did not show up, and I never did meet her. I presume she was too embarrassed to come to my office where I was in the power position and she was the one who wanted a job. Please, remember, today you are reading this book as an actor, but tomorrow, you may be an award-winning director. The same with that award-winning director. Tomorrow, he may be on skid row.

Today does not determine what tomorrow will bring. We read examples of that all the time. Multi-millionaire musicians, box office stars, television personalities are filing for bankruptcy. People are just not smart with their money or their egos. We read about big stars getting into fist-fights. Yes, the paparazzi can get out of hand. It is believed that they chased Lady Di to her death, but we don't read about it daily. It is usually a select few that we seem to hear about on a constant basis. Keep yourself in line.

If you are truly interested in the entertainment business and you want to make your living at it, then, by all means, don't let your ego get out of control. Make sure your head still fits through the door. People want to deal with nice actors, not pompous asses! We see them all the time. I get actors who walk into my Florida office and announce, "I'm from New York." I am not quite sure what response they are looking for after this declaration, but I usually say, "I'm from Florida." And then? It doesn't matter how much work you have under your belt or on your résumé, people will respond to you more than to a piece of paper listing your work.

An actor friend with whom I deal, works a lot, but not on a continuous basis. He may book many high profile commercials, TV shows, and movies all in the same several months and then nothing for a while. It's amazing to watch his ego go wild when he's working and then see how humble he becomes when the work slows down and he hasn't shot anything for a period of time. Frankly, I prefer to work with the humble guy. The humble guy doesn't curse. He laughs more, is available for lunches and dinners, and likes to come over and play with my little girl. The working guy—same guy—curses like a sailor. I suspect that's how they talk on the set. He gets way too busy to deal with anyone other than producers, directors and important clients.

All I am saying is to keep yourself in check. Watch that ego and watch that spending. Many successful people in all categories of our business maintain a balanced lifestyle, both personally and financially. It is possible. If you can do it, you'll be much happier in the long run.

Notes

38
How to Maintain a Healthy Lifestyle While Working in This Crazy Business

I believe that a book about auditioning must include a morsel about healthy living. Why is that? Maintaining clear thinking, lots of energy and a positive attitude and focus requires a healthy body. I encounter tens of thousands of actors yearly. I see them when they are healthy and when they are suffering. The number of actors unable to make castings due to various ailments amazes me. Most of these are stomach and intestine-related and could directly be attributed to stress and to the way the actor eats. The popular diseases I hear about from actors are ulcerative colitis, irritable bowel syndrome and Crohn's disease. It is staggering how much disease is out there in general, let alone amongst the talent pool.

I have practiced Macrobiotics for almost ten years. I've read about it for more than double that amount of time. When actors come to my office and see the way I eat, they always ask questions. During my lunch break on one of the weekend workshops I was teaching, a student came to talk to me. She saw me eating brown rice, beans and veggies and inquired about my diet. It seems she had taken steroids for a year or more to treat ulcerative colitis. Her doctor told her she would need this medication for the rest of her life. She always felt tired and her skin was a grayish color. She couldn't be too far from a bathroom and she no longer was able to dance, which had been her first love. I told her that by changing her eating and lifestyle to a Macrobiotic way of life, she could easily rectify that condition.

I told her about a weeklong program in which I had participated back in 1998, at the Kushi Institute in Becket, Massachusetts. I suggested she do that as well. She took my advice and she embraced the Macrobiotic way of eating and living. After many months of taking care of herself, she was able to stop all medication, to get the color back in her skin, to gain back all of the weight she had lost, and she could dance again.

Due to this business in the first place, she had been living on coffee, which eroded her stomach lining, on sugared foods such as donuts and muffins, and on fast foods filled with trans fatty acids, chemicals and preservatives. Her sleep habits were not normal, and she did nothing to nurture herself. When I met this girl, she was only twenty-two years of age. This is quite young for someone to start on this medical journey.

While on my health journey, I have watched how others conduct themselves in this business. I had an assistant in my company for many years that I watched go from size two to size sixteen and beyond. She drank about four to six giant-size diet sodas daily and always ate food prepared by a restaurant. Many people don't know that restaurant food is usually doused with salt to make it taste better. My assistant thought that eating sushi was eating well, but unless you order your sushi with brown rice or kitchen rice, you get regular sushi rice that is laden with sugar to improve taste. Daily, I advised her that this eating regimen would be her undoing. The large quantity of diet sodas that she consumed alone would hurt her. She always told me I didn't know what I was talking about. One morning, this forty-six year-old girl had a massive stroke that left her partially paralyzed, unable to work, talk, drive or to live a normal life.

When actors have been working on a set for many months at a time, they always seem to gain weight. When I asked one of these actors why this happens, he said, "Craft service." What is this mysterious *craft service*? It is the snacks put out on sets for people to munch on between meals. These snacks are usually unhealthy foods, like some form of candy, cookies and chips. Every once in a while you see fruit and veggies, but for the most part, the snacks are the definition of junk food. Craft service, or *crap service*, as it has been called, is just that—it's not very good for you.

No one holds a gun to actors' heads, telling them to eat that stuff. If you're working on a set and know you'll be hungry, bring a healthy snack for yourself. You don't have to eat set food. There are many ways you can take care of yourself while working on a set. Many times the food served is greasy, fried, quickly prepared, and full of chemicals and preservatives. I've spent many hours on sets, while working on a feature or a television series. Even though it's a little more work for me, I prepare my food in advance to assure I have good things to eat. If I have to be on the set in the early hours of the morning, I get up extra early to eat something healthy before I leave my house. This is all do-able! It just depends on how serious you are about your health and about feeling good.

One of the biggest contributors to ill health is sugar. Sugar is everywhere. They sneak it into our fast foods, our breakfast cereals, our breads—you name it. They sneak it into foods that would surprise you, and sugar can do a lot of damage to you as an actor. In his book

Let Food Be Thy Medicine, Alex Jack quotes researcher Paul Pitchford about sugar: "It weakens the mind, causing loss of memory and concentration, nervous disorders, shyness, violence, excessive or no talking, negative thought, paranoia and emotional upsets such as self pity, arguments, irritability." He continues, "People who stop eating sugar nearly always experience higher spirits, emotional stability, improved memory and speech, restful sleep and dreams, fewer colds and dental problems, more endurance and concentration and better health in general."

You are an actor. What are some of the most important components needed for your audition? Concentration. Improved memory. Less nerves. So, if you have an overabundance of the negative qualities listed above, you need to cut sugar out of your diet. Another excerpt from Alex Jack's book tells us that the average consumption of sugar between 1700 and 1800 ranged from four to eighteen pounds of sugar per person, per year. Today, the average intake per person, per year is one hundred and twenty-five pounds of sugar! That's a lot of sugar.

Many times when an actor comes in to audition for me, they are very nervous. Some of the symptoms are shaking, perspiring, dry mouth, lack of concentration and inability to hear. Diet and exercise can decrease these symptoms, if not eliminate them altogether. When an actor comes in to audition and they have any of the above conditions, I usually ask them what they ate before coming to my office. Often I hear *caffeine*, which can cause the jitters. I hear *salty foods* or *I smoked a cigarette*, both of which cause dry mouth. I tell you all of this because what you eat can contribute to the success or the demise of your audition.

I heard about a good actor who experienced such anxiety when auditioning that he went to his doctor for antidepressants. This made me so angry. That man didn't need antidepressants. He needed to clean up his diet and to work on some coping skills!

You have chosen to be an actor. Your passion is acting. Otherwise you would not be reading this book. Don't numb the experience by taking drugs. Clear out your mind by cleaning up your diet and start to exercise. Take a thirty minute walk on a daily basis to clear your mind. Oxygen to the brain can clear the mind. Deep, as opposed to shallow breathing, can really help you focus. Research yoga classes, guided meditations, exercise groups, Pilates, or anything else that you feel can help get your body back in shape. Once you get your body more healthy, you will see how clear your mind will become.

An actor on a television series sat around all day, drinking caffeinated coffee, while waiting to shoot his death scene. By the end of the day, when he finally shot his scene, his eye twitched from all the caffeine he'd consumed. They couldn't shoot him looking like he was already dead, and they ended up having to freeze the frame because his eye wouldn't stop twitching. The actor later told me he was sure that was due to the amount of caffeine he drank.

When your mind is sharper, your auditioning experience will be so much better. Don't wait! Start getting yourself in shape now for a better acting career.

Notes

39
Never Take No

We are coming to the end of this book and you've learned a great deal of valuable information. I believe this thirty-ninth morsel is very important, because even if you have everything down to a science, people will still say *no* to you. I always tell actors that they can never take no for an answer. You see, it is the job of the casting director or agent to say no. It is the job of the actor to convince us to change that answer.

As a casting director, I am bombarded by thousands of requests from actors and wanna-be actors to see them, audition them, and cast them. I cannot possibly see everyone who wants to see me. There are not enough hours in the day. I would never get any work done.

I was casting a movie called *Striptease*, starring Demi Moore. This was the first movie in which a female lead was paid the ridiculously high sum of $12 million. A lot of hoopla surrounded this project, and everyone wanted to work on the movie. I received almost six thousand pieces of mail from potential actors looking to work on this movie. I had to hire someone just to open and sort through this mail.

Seeing all those people would have been impossible, so my job was to say no to most and to see only the people I absolutely needed.

Your job is to get us to say *yes*. If we hang up on you, show up at our door. If we slam the door in your face, come down the chimney. If we close the chimney, climb in the window. This is all figuratively speaking, of course, but you need to get in to see us no matter how you can do it. If you don't, there are hundreds and thousands right behind you, waiting for the opportunity.

When I finished casting the last season of *Miami Vice* here in Miami, I had no job prospects. I did, however, have a mortgage and a car payment. I needed a job, and as we all know, DESPERATION IS A GREAT MOTIVATOR. I went out to Los Angeles with a plan to meet as many casting directors as possible who could refer work to me back here in Miami. My first target was the head of casting for one of the largest studios. Having just finished casting a very popular television series, I figured that was a good place to start.

I found the name of the woman who was the head of the casting department and I called her. Her assistant, the secretary, answered the phone. I knew that the most important person in any office is the secretary, so I really wanted to impress this woman. She was a very nice lady, who told me that the head of casting had just flown back from New York the night before, was swamped with work, and could not possibly come to the phone. I begged. NEVER BE ABOVE BEGGING! Finally, the secretary put her boss on the phone, who at first, was not very nice. She probably felt annoyed that the secretary had talked her into picking up the phone. She said she had the flu and jet lag and too much work on her desk, and she didn't have any time to meet me that week. I said I'd be in town the following week, as well, but she told me no, again. I could hear the misery in her voice, so I decided to play into it. I said how sorry I felt for her and that she must really feel lousy. I told her she really needed to be home in bed with a nice hot bowl of chicken soup and some good reading material, big pillows, and a remote control. She softened. She suggested that I mail in my résumé, and she gave me her address. I thanked her kindly, told her to feel better, and I hung up.

I was staying with my friend at his apartment in L.A., and when I hung up, I told him the story. Then I said I was going over to her office. My friend, an out-of-work actor, said, "You can't go over there. She'll throw you out." I pointed to the telephone and told him that she had already thrown me out, so I had nothing to lose. You see, WHEN YOU HAVE NOTHING, YOU HAVE NOTHING TO LOSE, right? He freaked out and told me that I didn't understand how it was done in L.A. I explained that I had no choice because I needed a job and that woman was someone who could help me achieve that.

Later that day, I got all dressed up for my interview. I first figured out what character I wanted to portray, what impression I wanted to make. When you are going to meet someone, whether it is an agent, casting director, old friend, whomever, there is a certain persona you want to convey, or there should be. You need to figure out how you want to be perceived. I wanted to be seen as very professional. I put on my skirt suit, stockings and heels, and I carried my nice leather briefcase. My hair and makeup were done in a natural way. I wore small pearl earrings and a conservative watch. I did not want to come across as a floozy or a slob. This was our first meeting, and as they say—I repeat again—you only have one chance to make a first impression.

I drove over to the studio building, where a gate and its guards blocked my entrance. I wondered how I would get past. Across the street from this intimidating site, I saw a smaller group of offices and decided to snoop around there. As it turned out, those offices were for some of the employees of this studio, as well, just not for the more important people. I figured I would recognize one name, so I parked my car and walked up and down the hallways until I saw a name familiar to me. I walked in, but the person whose name I recognized was not there. Her assistant was. As I keep saying, the most important person in any office is the assistant, the secretary! I asked the assistant where her boss was, and she told me she was out to lunch. I said I needed to see someone across the street and that I would come back later. I asked if she would be so kind as to call the guard at that gate to leave my name, so I could get in. She said *yes*. I was in!

This next part may sound like I'm making it up, but believe me, I'm not that creative. This actually happened. I drove through the gate and parked my car. I walked up to the glass doors of the building and looked through to see a guard at a sign-in podium. I had no appointment, and in order to get into the elevator, I needed to get past that guard. With all of the confidence I could muster, I walked with conviction through those doors, looked at him like I did this every day, and said, "Good morning!" Then I marched myself past the guard and into the elevator. Whew! I did this with so much confidence that the guard probably didn't want to embarrass himself by stopping me to ask who I was or where I was going. Since I was dressed in a very professional manner, I looked like I belonged.

When I got to the floor where the head casting director was, I approached a desk. I asked the young lady there if this was indeed the area where I needed to be and she confirmed that it was. I asked her name and discovered that she was the nice secretary from my original phone call. When she asked who I was, I stood up straight and tall and announced that I was Lori Wyman. The next thing that happened amazed me, so that when I tell this story even now, I still find it hard to believe. After I gave her my name, she jumped up from her seat and said, "I've been looking all over for you!" That certainly wasn't the response I was expecting, but I was pleased to hear it.

You see, after I had spoken to the main casting director, she decided to go home, since she felt so sick. When she got to the elevator, she ran into a man who was producing a television series down in South Florida. She asked him how he was doing with his Florida casting director, and he said he was looking for someone. She told him that I was in town and that I had just finished casting the last season of *Miami Vice* in Miami. He asked her to have her secretary call his to set up an appointment. She told her secretary to find me and she couldn't leave that day until she did. I hadn't left a phone number, so her secretary didn't know where to find me. There is no such thing as coincidence now, is there? I met with this wonderful man and ended up casting the next season of the *B.L. Stryker* series in a lovely town called Jupiter, Florida.

What would have happened if I had taken no for an answer? I never would have spoken to the head of casting for that studio. She never would have known I was in town and she never would have suggested that I was available to that executive producer. As for my out-of-work actor friend, he never got work as an actor because his dad paid all of his bills every month and he wasn't hungry. He took no for an answer on a consistent basis and never got anywhere with his acting career. You have a choice. It just depends on what you really want. If this career is a passion of yours, if it is a must for you and you have to make it to eat and survive, you cannot take no for an answer.

Notes

40

The Summation

So everybody, you have read, from start to finish, how to get into this business, what to do when you're in this business, thoughts of a casting director, what goes on behind the scenes, the tools that you need—how to win friends and influence people, as they say. The most important thing that I must impress upon you is: Follow Your Dream. You have read this book because you dream of becoming an actor. So often, when a parent hears their child wants to be an actor, they say, "Oh, no, get a stable career." I'm here to tell you that acting is a passion and you must follow the dream of your passion.

I teach a weekend workshop in which, on Sunday mornings, I ask the actors, "Has anyone won the lottery?" because Florida has a Saturday night lottery. Of course, they say, "No, we haven't won the lottery." Not yet. "Let me ask you another question," I continue. "If you did win the lottery, would you not still be here?" Every actor says they would absolutely still be in the class, because acting is not a job, it's a passion.

Ask the average person, "What would you do if you won the lottery?" and what does the person say? "I'd quit my job." If you ask an actor, "What would you do if you won the lottery?" they say, "I'd move to Los Angeles. I'd take more acting courses. I'd produce my play. I'd produce my film. I'd go to New York. I'd study." Anybody who is an actor would not say, "I'd quit my job."

You have purchased this book because you have a passion, because you have a dream. Please, take to heart the words that I have imparted to you throughout this book. Learn them, study them and incorporate them into your career. Live the dream. Pursue your passion.

I thank you for reading this. I thank you for going on this journey with me, and I wish you much success in your career.

About the Author

Lori S. Wyman, C.S.A., an Emmy and two-time ARTIOS Award nominee, known by her students as "Actor Whisperer," has worked in casting since 1979. After beginning her career as a talent agent, Lori became the in-house casting director for the hit television series *Miami Vice*, before starting her own company, Lori Wyman Casting. For over two decades, she has been considered one of the most prominent casting directors in the Southeast. Lori has spent thousands of hours casting major television series and feature films, enabling her to understand the entire audition process. In 1985, at the insistence of actors who auditioned for her, Lori began teaching her successful auditioning for film and television workshops.

CPSIA information can be obtained at www.ICGtesting.com
Printed in the USA
LVOW08s2251030315

429111LV00004B/6/P